Company's Coming

LEARN TO

Make Cards With Photos

Limited Edition, page 96

www.companyscoming.com
visit our website

Front Cover: Maple Leaf, page 90

Learn to Make Cards With Photos

Copyright © Company's Coming Publishing Limited

First Printing August 2009

Library and Archives Canada Cataloguing in Publication
Learn to make cards with photos.
(Company's coming crafts)
Includes index.
ISBN 978-1-897477-14-4
1. Greeting cards. 2. Photographs. 3. Paper work. 4. Handicraft.
I. Title: Make cards with photos. II. Series: Company's coming crafts
TT872.C37 2008   745.594'1   C2008-907755-5

Published by
Company's Coming Publishing Limited
2311-96 Street
Edmonton, Alberta, Canada T6N 1G3
Tel: 780-450-6223   Fax: 780-450-1857
www.companyscoming.com

Company's Coming is a registered trademark owned by Company's Coming Publishing Limited

Printed in China

The Company's Coming Story

Jean Paré grew up with an understanding that family, friends and home cooking are the key ingredients for a good life. A mother of four, Jean worked as a professional caterer for 18 years, operating out of her home kitchen. During that time, she came to appreciate quick and easy recipes that call for everyday ingredients. In answer to mounting requests for her recipes, Company's Coming cookbooks were born, and Jean moved on to a new chapter in her career.

Company's Coming founder Jean Paré

Just as Company's Coming continues to promote the tradition of home cooking, the same is now true with crafting. Like good cooking, great craft results depend upon easy-to-follow instructions, readily available materials and enticing photographs of the finished products. Also like cooking, crafting is meant to be enjoyed in the home or cottage. Company's Coming Crafts, then, is a natural extension from the kitchen into the family room or den.

In the beginning, Jean worked from a spare bedroom in her home, located in the small prairie town of Vermilion, Alberta, Canada. The first Company's Coming cookbook, *150 Delicious Squares*, was an immediate bestseller. Today, with well over 150 titles in print, Company's Coming has earned the distinction of publishing Canada's most popular cookbooks. The company continues to gain new supporters by adhering to Jean's "Golden Rule of Cooking"—Never share a recipe you wouldn't use yourself. It's an approach that has worked—millions of times over!

Company's Coming cookbooks are distributed throughout Canada, the United States, Australia and other international English-language markets. French and Spanish language editions have also been published. Sales to date have surpassed 25 million copies with no end in sight. Familiar and trusted in home kitchens around the world, Company's Coming cookbooks are highly regarded both as kitchen workbooks and as family heirlooms.

Because Company's Coming operates a test kitchen and not a craft shop, we've partnered with a major North American craft content publisher to assemble a variety of craft compilations exclusively for us. Our editors have been involved every step of the way. You can see the excellent results for yourself in the book you're holding.

Company's Coming Crafts are for everyone—whether you're a beginner or a seasoned pro. What better gift could you offer than something you've made yourself? In these hectic days, people still enjoy crafting parties; they bring family and friends together in the same way a good meal does. Company's Coming is proud to support crafters with this new creative book series.

We hope you enjoy these easy-to-follow, informative and colourful books, and that they inspire your creativity. So, don't delay—get crafty!

TABLE OF CONTENTS

Feeling Crafty? Get Creative! 6 • Foreword 7 • General Instructions 8 • Crafting With Photos 11

Bon Voyage, 28

Decorating Eggs, 48

Lovely Baby Girl, 36

TABLE OF CONTENTS

Snowy Morning, 84

Relax, 112

Fall Harvest, 80

Feeling Crafty? Get Creative!

Each 160-page book features easy-to-follow, step-by-step instructions and full-page colour photographs of every project. Whatever your crafting fancy, there's a Company's Coming Creative Series craft book to match!

Beading: Beautiful Accessories in Under an Hour

Complement your wardrobe, give your home extra flair or add an extra-special personal touch to gifts with these quick and easy beading projects. Create any one of these special crafts in an hour or less.

Knitting: Easy Fun for Everyone

Take a couple of needles and some yarn and see what beautiful things you can make! Learn how to make fashionable sweaters, comfy knitted blankets, scarves, bags and other knitted crafts with these easy to intermediate knitting patterns.

Card Making: Handmade Greetings for All Occasions

Making your own cards is a fun, creative and inexpensive way of letting someone know you care. Stamp, emboss, quill or layer designs in a creative and unique card with your own personal message for friends or family.

Patchwork Quilting

In this book full of throws, baby quilts, table toppers, wall hangings—and more—you'll find plenty of beautiful projects to try. With the modern fabrics available, and the many practical and decorative applications, patchwork quilting is not just for Grandma!

Crocheting: Easy Blankets, Throws & Wraps

Find projects perfect for decorating your home, for looking great while staying warm or for giving that one-of-a-kind gift. A range of simple but stunning designs make crocheting quick, easy and entertaining.

Sewing: Fun Weekend Projects

Find a wide assortment of easy and attractive projects to help you create practical storage solutions, decorations for any room or just the right gift for that someone special. Create table runners, placemats, baby quilts, pillows and more!

For more information about Company's Coming craft books, visit our website, www.companyscoming.com

FOREWORD

Creating handmade greeting cards is a pastime that's taking the crafting world by storm. Sending handcrafted greetings is a way of sharing not only our creative passion, but with every card creation, we share a bit of ourselves. We put careful thought and planning into designing the perfect cards for our loved ones and friends, because we want them to know that the cards were created specifically with them in mind. I have to remember the old saying, "A picture's worth a thousand words," when it comes to making cards with photos. There's simply no better way to incorporate the most personal expression in your greeting cards than with photographs.

In our Life's Events chapter, peanut shells are used as a complementary embellishment on a fun-loving birthday card. Use close-up photos to create adorable birth announcements, and see how copies of a photo can be turned into a stunning focal point with tea bag folding on our Wedding Bouquet project.

The Holidays chapter will encourage you to remember that every day's a holiday with fun photo cards. We've included creative holiday projects for occasions such as Valentine's Day, Easter and Christmas—and many more.

In the Seasons chapter, see how seasonal photos inspire card designs. Springtime photos of bright blossoms work perfectly on all-occasion cards. Photos from the beach, or a simple shot of a juicy piece of watermelon, make great summer party invitations. Cards crafted with photos of fall leaves and pumpkins are the best way to announce the arrival of autumn, and a photo of snow-covered pines or holiday decorations creates the ideal theme for wintertime cards.

In our chapter titled Just Because, see how a simple photo can be used to create a card that's simply beautiful. A photo of wildflowers or a favourite pet is used to say, "I'm thinking of you." A shot of a roadside sign makes a real statement on a card of encouragement. There's no better way to personalize a greeting card than with photos of family members or friends.

Choose from 48 creative designs featuring various techniques and tools. Learn to colourize a black and white photo with special photo markers, calling attention to a particular detail. Punch out or trim a specific portion of a photo and mount it on foam adhesive squares, creating a strong focal point. Use embossing die cuts to add a bit of subtle dimension to a photo. Cut a photo into small squares and reassemble on a card front to create a mosaic-style card. The techniques and creative uses for photos on cards are endless!

To get you started on creating stunning photo cards, we will walk you through the basics and more involved techniques of crafting with photos. You'll learn about tools and adhesives that work best with photos, unique ways to add colour to photos and helpful tips for achieving different effects with photo-editing software.

30 Already?, page 24

GENERAL INSTRUCTIONS

Embellishments

If you are not already a pack rat, it is time to start! Embellish projects with stickers, eyelets, brads, nail heads, wire, beads, iron-on ribbon and braid, memorabilia and printed ephemera.

Embossing

Dry embossing: Use a light source, stencil, card stock and stylus tool. Add colour, or leave raised areas plain.

Heat embossing: Use embossing powder, ink, card stock and a heat tool to create raised designs and textures. Powders come in a wide range of colours. Fine grain is called "detail" and heavier is called "ultrathick." Embossing powders will not stick to most dye inks—use pigment inks or special clear embossing inks for best results.

Cutting & Tearing

Craft knife, cutting mat: Must-have tools. Mat protects work surface, keeps blades from getting dull.

Measure and mark: Diagrams show solid lines for cutting, dotted lines for folding.

Other cutters: Guillotine and rotary-blade paper cutters, oval and circle cutters, cutters that cut unusual shapes via a gear or cam system, swivel-blade knives that cut along the channels of plastic templates, and die-cutting machines (large or small in size and price). Markers that draw as they cut.

Punches: Available in hundreds of shapes and sizes ranging from 1⁄16 inch to over 3 inches (use for eyelets, lettering, dimensional punch art and embellishments). Also punches for two-ring, three-ring, coil, comb and disk binding.

Scissors: Long and short blades that cut straight or a pattern. Scissors with nonstick coating are ideal for cutting adhesive sheets and tape. Bonsai scissors are best for cutting rubber or heavy board. Consider comfort—large holes for fingers, soft grips.

Tearing: Tear paper for collage, special effects, layering on cards, scrapbook pages and more. Wet a small paintbrush with water then brush across paper where tear is desired; tear along the wet line for a deckle edge.

Glues & Adhesives

Basics: Each glue or adhesive is formulated for a particular use and specified surfaces. Read the label and carefully follow directions, especially those that involve personal safety and health.

Foam tape: Adds dimension.

Glue dots, adhesive sheets and cartridge type: machines Quick grab, no drying time needed.

Glue pens: Fine-line control.

Glue sticks: Wide coverage.

Repositionable products: Useful for stencils and temporary holding.

Pens & Markers

Choose inks: (permanent, watercolour, metallic, etc.), **colours** (sold by sets or individually), **and nibs** (fine point, calligraphy, etc.) **to suit the project.** For journals and scrapbooks, make sure inks are permanent and fade-resistant.

Store pens and markers flat unless the manufacturer says otherwise.

Scoring & Folding

Folding: Mountain folds—up, valley folds—down. Most patterns will have different types of dotted lines to denote mountain or valley folds.

Tools: Scoring tool and bone folder. (Fingernails will scar the surface of the paper.)

Measuring

Rulers: A metal straightedge for cutting with a craft knife (a must-have tool). Match the length of the ruler to the project (shorter rulers are easier to use when working on smaller projects).

Quilter's grid ruler: Use to measure squares and rectangles.

Paper & Card Stock

Card stock: Heavier and stiffer than paper. A sturdy surface for cards, boxes, ornaments.

Paper: Lighter-weight surfaces used for drawing, stamping, collage.

Storage and organization: Store paper flat and away from moisture. Arrange by colour, size or type. Keep your scraps for collage projects.

Types: Handmade, milled, marbled, mulberry, origami, embossed, glossy, matte, botanical inclusions, vellum, parchment, preprinted, tissue and more.

Stamping

Direct-to-paper (DTP): Use ink pad, sponge or stylus tool to apply ink instead of a rubber stamp.

Inks: Available in pads and re-inker bottles. Types include dye and pigment, permanent, waterproof and fade resistant or archival, chalk finish, fast drying, slow drying, rainbow and more. Read the labels to determine what is best for a project or surface.

Make stamps: Carve rubber, erasers, carving blocks, vegetables. Heat Magic Stamp foam blocks to press against textures. Stamp found objects such as leaves and flowers, keys and coins, etc.

Stamps: Sold mounted on wood, acrylic or foam, or unmounted (rubber part only), made from vulcanized rubber, acrylic or foam.

Store: Flat and away from light and heat.

Techniques: Tap the ink onto the stamp (using the pad as the applicator) or tap the stamp onto the ink pad. Stamp with even hand pressure (no rocking) for best results. For very large stamps, apply ink with a brayer. Colour the surface of a stamp with watercolour markers (several colours), huff with breath to keep the colours moist, then stamp; or lightly spray with water mist before stamping for a very different effect.

Unmounted stamps: Mount temporarily on acrylic blocks with Scotch Poster Tape on one surface (nothing on the rubber stamp) or one of the other methods (hook-and-loop fastener, paint-on adhesives, cling plastic).

CRAFTING WITH PHOTOS

Introduction

If a picture is worth a thousand words, then the projects you can create with your photos are priceless! Don't leave your pictures in a shoebox or put them on a shelf to sort through someday—use those wonderful photographs to create something grand.

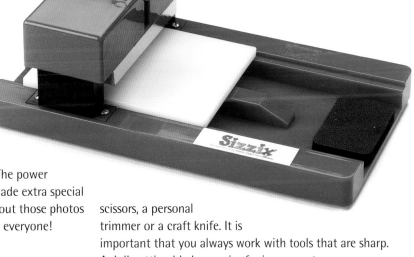

You can have fun with photo transferring, organizing a photo mosaic, colourizing a black-and-white photo to capture the romance of years gone by and even creating an interesting collage to celebrate your life. The power of the visual medium of photography is made extra special when you add the spirit of creativity. Get out those photos and start a project that will be enjoyed by everyone!

Handy Tools

The list of photo-crafting tools could go on forever, but there are a few that are vital for any project. The first is a sharp cutting tool, which can be traditional scissors, a personal trimmer or a craft knife. It is important that you always work with tools that are sharp. A dull cutting blade or pair of scissors can tear or mar a photo—especially photos that are printed on home printers. These are very functional tools and a must for photo crafting.

Cutting tools can also be just plain fun! There are dozens of decorative scissors, hand paper punches and die-cutting plates to help you create interesting, exciting edges and corners for your photos. You can choose from deckled edges to postage-stamp edges to traditional zigzag edges to add variety to your projects. Paper punches come in every size and shape from apples to zebras! Dies can usually be found at craft or scrapbook stores where you pay per cut of the die. Dies are available in even more shapes and sizes than hand punches.

Adhesives are important to any craft project. It's best to coordinate the adhesive to the materials you are using. Photos can be attached in a variety of ways, from liquid glue to any of the many types of tape that are available. If you are adhering anything heavy or nonporous to your photo project, you'll need to consider a specialty paper glue or a jewellry glue, both of which are designed to hold heavier items to a surface. Many artists and crafters are incorporating metal and glass

into their photo crafts, and this technique calls for a stronger glue. If you are only working with lightweight embellishments and paper, then most white glues will do the trick. Archival, heirloom and scrapbooking projects should use a glue labelled as acid-free to prevent eventual deterioration of the photographs.

Pens, inks, coloured or watercolour pencils, markers, chalk and paint all add colour and interest to photo crafts. Feel free to use them with splash and flash; however, if creating an archival or heirloom design, keep in mind that there are acid-free pens, coloured pencils, inks, markers and paint available. Most of these supplies are indeed acid-free, but not all manufacturers go through the testing process. Call the manufacturer if you have archival-quality questions. The same goes for most printer inks; most are acid-free, but are not always labelled as such.

Other handy tools include stencils and templates. A huge variety of clever and inspiring stencils and templates are available at art- and craft–supply stores, and a quick search on the Internet will provide dozens of free stencils and templates to choose from. You can cut an interesting shape, emboss a raised image and fold a beautiful flower, all with the help of these tools.

Just a Reminder

You probably have a few older photographs in your collection. It is important to remember that if the photo doesn't have a negative, you might want to craft with a copy of that photo, not the original. Old photos with charming sepia tones or hand tinting are great to craft with, but often are one-of-a-kind family mementoes. Keep the original photograph intact and make a few copies to craft with.

Digital or the Old-Fashioned Way?

It doesn't really matter anymore if you use photos taken with film or photos printed at home from your digital camera. The key is getting the best quality print you can.

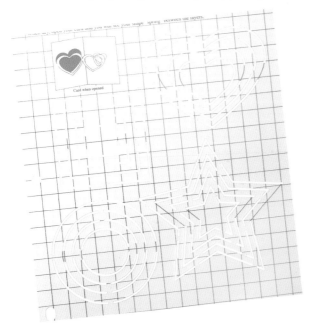

If you are working with an actual photograph rather than a photocopied print, you need quality photo paper and a quality printer. Photo paper is easy to find for home printers, but home printer quality still doesn't quite match that of a commercial photo developer. You need to decide what you prefer for each individual project you undertake. Sometimes a photo print from your home computer system is fine, while there may be other projects for which you'll prefer to have a professionally printed photo.

Tips for Photographs

To create great photo craft projects, you need to start with great photos! Here are some tips that leading professional photographers pass along to camera enthusiasts.

Know your camera. Read your camera manual and refer to it if you have any problems. It is very important that you know what all the buttons do and what features are available. Most are there for a good reason and to give

eye reducer. According to a leading camera manufacturer, the No. 1 flash mistake is taking pictures beyond the range of the flash. Photos taken beyond the maximum flash range will be too dark. As a general rule most cameras have a maximum flash range of less than 15 feet. You can find the flash range in the camera manual.

Get down (or up) to the photo subject's eye level. This is especially important when photographing children and pets. You may have to kneel, bend, hunch or stand on a stool, but the effort is worth it. Being at eye level gives a warm, personal feel to the photo without the necessity of the subject looking directly at the camera lens. In fact, some of the most intimate photos are those with the subject looking off to either side of the camera lens.

When you look through the camera viewfinder, it is natural for you to focus all of your attention on the subject. However, your camera is not doing the same. Standing too far away can lead to your subject getting lost in the landscape or background. Move closer so you can see more detail. Or, if your camera has a zoom lens, let the camera do the work by zooming closer. Next time you take a picture of your best friend, let her face fill the viewfinder and you'll get some amazing results.

you the best possible photos. The next step is to practice and keep your camera handy for any photo opportunity.

Do more than just aim and click your camera. Take charge and get the photo you want. As you look through the viewfinder, take time to really see what you are looking at. Ask people to move closer together for a better shot. Tell Grandpa Ralph to lean slightly to the left or right. Add a prop. Remove a hat. Do whatever it takes to make the photo better, tell a story or make you smile.

The most vital part of every photograph you take is light. Lighting affects the appearance of everything you photograph. Harsh light can make your subjects squint and grimace. Not enough light results in shadowy darkness. If the lighting is not right, move yourself or your subject. Check the settings on your camera and adjust for bright light, cloudiness, incandescent or fluorescent light, and moonlight.

Learn when to use your flash to fill in with supplemental light and when you should use the red-

Hold the camera steady with both hands and gently push the shutter button down. Nothing can blur a great photo faster than unsteady hands. Consider using a tripod for posed shots.

Most photos are taken with a horizontal frame. It's natural and done without thinking. Why not shoot a photo vertically every now and then? Many things look better when a vertical picture is taken, such as friends standing around a birthday cake, or tall buildings. This adds variety to the photos by showing different lines, shapes, forms and perspective. Next time you get ready to shoot a photo, take a few extra seconds and turn your camera sideways. You might get a better shot.

A plain background gives focus to the subject you are photographing. When you look through the camera viewfinder, learn to pay attention to the area surrounding your subject. Make sure no trees grow from the head of your grandson and no wires seem to be stretching from the sides of Aunt Barb. Keep your photo backgrounds free from clutter.

To avoid the dreaded bull's-eye syndrome, remember the rule of thirds. Divide your photo frame into nine equal segments. Instead of having the focus of your photo in the centre of the nine squares, place it off-centre in any of the remaining eight. If you photograph the horizon line at the bottom third of your frame, the focus of the photo will be the magnificent sunset. If the horizon line is at the top third of the camera frame, the focus will be the craggy mountains, with the sunset as an accent. The same rule applies to photographing people or pets. Keeping the subject a bit off-centre adds to the variety of lines, shapes, forms, balance and harmony of the photograph, which in turn will create more exciting photos for your craft projects.

Black-and-white photos are known to have a longer life than most colour photographs and are often more dramatic, so include black-and-white film in your picture taking. Some digital cameras have a

black-and-white (greyscale) mode. You also have an opportunity to include black-and-white style when you scan a photo by using photo-editing software that includes a greyscale feature.

Adding Colour to a Black-and-White Photo

Colouring a black-and-white photo can add a special tint to your photo crafts. It is not as hard as you might imagine it to be. The finished effect is nostalgic and romantic. You may find some original hand-coloured photos among your older treasured family photos. These photos were probably hand-coloured by professional photographers using oil paints. This technique is still used, and oil-paint products are available at art, craft and photography shops. However, modern products have taken much of the tedium and mystery out of this technique. You no longer have to be a professional artist or even have any artistic ability to hand-colour photos.

The first rule to remember is never hand-colour an original black-and-white photo. Have a copy made on photo paper. Remember that any negative can be developed into a black-and-white photo, and a colour photo can be printed in black and white at a photo developer or by using your computer.

That's right, even your colour negatives can be processed into black-and-white photos. Once the film has been developed, just ask your developer to make some copies in black-and-white. Most shops will not be able to do this process in-house, but it is well worth the extra day or two it takes to obtain black-and-white prints to hand-colour.

There are three basic methods used to hand-colour an actual photo. The first involves an oil paint, as previously described. This method takes some practice and the paint is applied by brush or paint pen. The second method uses acrylic paint or tints and is applied in the same manner. The final method, and by far the easiest, is to use markers specifically developed to hand-colour black-and-white photos. Depending on what brand of products is used, you may have to sponge a solution onto the photo to soften the top layer, making it more receptive to colour. You'll then apply the colour. You may have to use an aerosol finish on the photo once completed to preserve the colour.

Photo-colouring markers provide very transparent tinting. Add colour in a circular motion, and apply layer upon layer of colour until the desired intensity is reached. Experiment with different colours. Many manufacturers carry stock colours that are close to the original hues used by professionals in days of old. Many manufacturers also include modern colours in their palettes.

You can also use coloured pencils to add soft colour to photos. Photocopy the print (if it is a black-and-white print, copy it on a colour copier to get richer grey tones), then add subtle strokes to add touches of colour. If you have your print copied onto a heavy card stock or watercolour paper (printable watercolour papers are available at most art or computer stores), you can also use watercolour pencils to give the effect of hand-colouring. You'll softly stroke colour into one area of the image and then, using a small damp paintbrush or waterbrush, you'll add just a touch of water to allow the pencil colour to flow or blend, as watercolours do so beautifully.

Magical Mosaics

You've probably seen beautiful mosaics used to create stepping-stones, tabletops, candleholders and wall art, but did you ever think of creating a mosaic with your photos? Somehow all the little pieces add up to big results! You can create your own mosaic by selecting the photos you want to include. Decide on how big you want each "tile" to be and start cutting! Large or small pieces do give different effects, so you may want to look through some photo-crafting books or do an Internet search for inspiration.

Give yourself plenty of working area, as you will want to keep some kind of order to the photo pieces. Once you have enough photos cut to fill in your surface you can start gluing—use a paper glue or double-sided tape. Leave a hint of a border or space between the photo pieces as you adhere each to a heavyweight background paper. You can use several photos or have a single photo enlarged. If you don't feel comfortable enough to "wing it" on your own, there are photo mosaic templates available at craft, scrapbooking and

Internet stores. Photos take on a different feel when cut up and then pieced together again.

Weave an Image

Weaving with strips from a photo is a unique way to add dimension and pattern to a photo-crafting design. Most of us learned the basics of weaving in grade school while creating placemats and valentine hearts that only our moms could really appreciate! The easiest technique to learn (or relearn) is the process of "over one, under one."

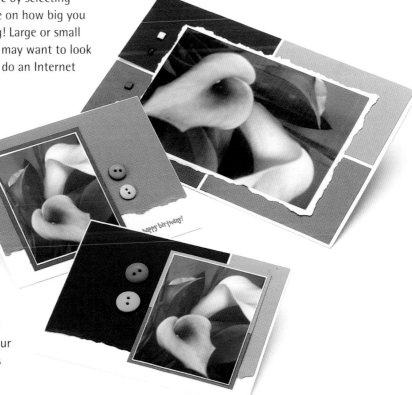

Here are a few weaving terms to become familiar with:

Loom: The frame used for weaving the piece.

Warp: The pieces that run from top to bottom (up and down).

Weft: The pieces than run across the warp (side to side).

Web: The single or whole piece created by weaving.

You'll need two identical photos, a personal trimmer or craft knife with ruler and self-healing cutting mat, and adhesive. The first photo will act as the loom as well as the warp. On the back of the photo, measure and mark ¼ inch, ½ inch or 1 inch (depending on the size of the photo) from what will be the top and both sides. Do not cut beyond these marks or your loom will fall apart. The warp pieces can be cut straight or curved, with all of them the same width or different widths. Cut the weft strips from the second photo (straight or curved). To make it easier, you can draw and number the curved pieces on the back before cutting them.

Begin weaving the first row by placing one strip of weft over one warp and under the next warp, and repeat to the end of the row. The second row starts with placing a weft strip under one warp and over the next warp; repeat to the end of the row. Keep the weft strips pushed toward the top of the loom. Alternate row one and row two until the web is complete. Secure woven ends with a touch of glue. Now you are ready to use your woven photo as is or as an element of scrapbooking, card making, paper art, collage and other fun creations.

Delightful Decoupage

This traditional technique can be applied to photo crafting with excellent results. You can decoupage a photo or a photocopied photo. Make sure when you are using photocopies that you always test a small area of the photocopy to make sure the ink is permanent.

Decoupage is traditionally done by adhering a print (in this case a photo) to a surface, usually wood. The wooden piece should be well prepared by sanding away rough edges and making sure all dust and dirt is wiped away. You'll also need a paintbrush, decoupage medium or sealer.

Apply a thin film of the decoupage medium to the wooden surface and place the photo on top. Gently press the photo, making sure there are no bumps, wrinkles or air bubbles underneath. Apply a second coat of decoupage medium, covering the entire surface, including the top of the photo.

Add several more coats of decoupage medium, allowing each coat to dry completely.

Decoupage can also be applied to paper and glass surfaces, but decoupage medium will not permanently adhere to most plastics.

Wild & Wacky Effects

If you enjoy working with a computer, many software programs with photo-editing applications include a wonderful creative tool called a filter. The filter can be applied to an entire image or part of an image. Filters can be fairly simple effects used to mimic traditional

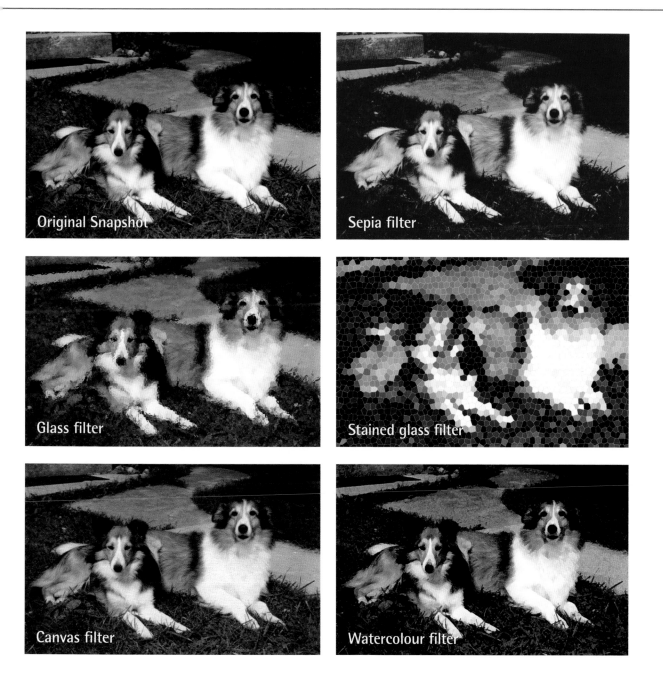

Original Snapshot

Sepia filter

Glass filter

Stained glass filter

Canvas filter

Watercolour filter

photographic filters (which are pieces of coloured glass or gelatine placed over the lens to absorb specific wavelengths of light), or they can be complex programs used to create astounding artistic effects. Using filters is a creative way to alter photos for crafting.

You can create 3-D effects, instant sepia or aging, watercolour, coloured foil, kaleidoscope or even a linen texture for your photos, all with a click of a mouse! The photos can be printed out on a variety of surfaces including watercolour paper, fabric, acetate transparencies, handmade paper, specialty papers, and of course, photo paper. Most software allows you to temporarily apply the filter to your scanned or digital photo so that you can see if you like it before saving it as a permanent file. Remember to always keep the original file untouched. You can do this by saving the filtered photo under a different file name.

Copyright Issues

Thinking of selling your photo crafts? If you are using your own photos that have been taken by you, a friend or someone in your family, you have nothing to worry about when it comes to copyright laws.

Professional photographers, however, own all the rights to photographs (even though you have purchased the photographs themselves), and you may not use their photographs for commercial use. In other words, you may not sell for profit anything using their photos. You must request permission from a photographer to use a photo and you must get a release form from him or her to do so.

Did You Know?

People immediately look at another human in a photo even if the person is very small in the frame. Our attention will go to anything alive as opposed to something inanimate. The hierarchy of attention is humans over animals, animals over plants.

Colours draw our attention, and the warm shades of red, yellow and orange will jump out of a background of cool-tone colours like blue and green. Even a small subject will dominate if it's different from its surroundings. It could be its colour, brightness or the direction it's facing. Anything that's isolated from everything else will draw attention to itself.

No matter what else is in the scene, the eye is irresistibly drawn to the lightest, brightest area. That's why any bright blob of light or bit of paper in the background is distracting. All other things being equal, the eye will go to the area of highest contrast. The eye will go to the subject that's in sharpest focus.

Can you crop Polaroid photographs? Yes and no! Cutting an older Polaroid photograph releases harmful chemicals from inside the image. As an alternative, you can place a frame made of acid-free paper over the top of the photograph, hiding the white borders. According to the manufacturer, photos made from film manufactured after 2003 can be cut without problems.

What's With The Paper?

Paper is a wonderful medium to use in photo crafting, but not all paper is the same. Here is a quick review of some papers you might like to use while creating with your photos.

Acetate: thin, flexible sheet of transparent plastic

Board: paper generally used for file folders, displays and postcards

Bond: paper generally used for writing, printing and photocopying

Buffered: made in an acid environment and then buffered on the surface to obtain a required pH

Cardboard: general term for stiff, bulky paper such as index, tag or Bristol

Coated: papers with a finish or coating that can be glossy or matte

Corrugated: fluted paper between sheets of paper or cardboard, or the fluted paper by itself

Dry gum: label paper or sheet of paper with glue on one side that can be activated by water

Handmade: sheet of paper made individually by hand using a mold and deckle

Index: lightweight board paper for writing and easy erasure

Mulberry: Made from the bark of the Paper Mulberry tree, this handmade paper contains coarse fibres that create a feathery look when the paper is torn or ripped.

Origami: very lightweight paper designed to crease or fold well

Parchment: paper that imitates writing "papers" made from animal skins

Quilling: lightweight paper, usually brightly coloured, cut into very thin strips that are rolled into coils and shaped

Rice: A misnomer that is applied to lightweight Oriental papers, the name may be derived from the rice sizing once used in Japanese papermaking.

Tissue: thin, translucent, lightweight paper

Vellum: stiff, translucent paper available clear, coloured, printed or embossed

Velveteen: paper with velvet nap and feel

Watercolour: Hot press is used for stamping because it is smooth; cold press is bumpy and is used mostly for painting. It has a high wet strength, meaning it doesn't lose strength when water is absorbed.

Waterleaf: paper with little or no sizing, making it very absorbent.

GO NUTS!

Save those peanut shells to use as unique embellishments on this light-hearted birthday card.

Design | Karen Robinson

Materials

Card stock: brown, light brown, beige
Brown squares printed paper
Beige paper
Digital photo of a squirrel or photo from a magazine
Peanut in shell
Rust raffia
Alphabet rubber stamps
Black dye ink pad
Brown chalk
6 epoxy square stickers
Gold jump rings: 2 (9-10mm), 2 (4-5mm)
Envelope template to fit a 4¾ x 6⅜-inch card
4 gold mini round brads
¹⁄₁₆-inch hole punch
Paintbrush
Paper piercer or awl
Needle-nose pliers
Sewing machine with brown all-purpose thread
Paper glue
Decoupage medium
Computer and printer

Instructions

Form a 4¾ x 6⅜-inch side-fold card from brown card stock. Adhere a 4¾ x 4-inch piece of light brown card stock to card front ¾ inch from top. Cut a 3 x 6⅜-inch piece of squares printed paper; adhere to card ½ inch from left edge of card. Zigzag stitch along left edge of paper.

Print photo on beige card stock; trim photo to approximately 2½ x 2½ inches. Chalk edges. Adhere image to right side of card, referring to photo for placement. Zigzag stitch around photo.

Stamp "GO NUTS" inside squares on square printed paper on card; attach a square sticker on top of each letter. Use a computer to generate, or hand-print, "ON YOUR BIRTHDAY" on beige card stock; cut a 4¾ x ⁹⁄₁₆-inch strip around sentiment. Chalk edges and adhere to bottom edge of light brown card stock on card. Punch a ¹⁄₁₆-inch hole through both ends of sentiment strip and in top corners of light brown rectangle on card; insert brads.

Carefully split peanut shell in half; brush inside and outside of one half of shell with decoupage medium. Let dry. Pierce a small hole on each end of shell; attach small jump rings to peanut shell. Attach larger jump rings to small jump rings. Tie raffia around shell into a bow; adhere shell to centre bottom of card. Pierce a small hole in fold of card ¾ inch from bottom; thread raffia through hole and tie onto both larger jump rings; trim raffia ends.

Use template to trace and cut an envelope from beige paper; score and fold to form envelope flaps. Adhere side and bottom flaps together. Use top envelope flap as a template to trace and cut a piece of brown squares printed paper to fit; adhere paper to envelope flap. Zigzag stitch around edges of top envelope flap. ■

GO NUTS

ON YOUR BIRTHDAY

Go Nuts!
Printed paper from Doodlebug Design Inc.; stickers from K&Company; template from Provo Craft/ Coluzzle; decoupage medium from Delta Creative Inc.

30 ALREADY?

*Photos of common roadside signs
become the focal point on this
fun birthday greeting card.*

Design | Alice Golden

Materials

5 x 6½-inch white card with envelope
White card stock
Red scuffed printed paper
Photo of "30" road sign
2 black elastic cords with attached fasteners
4 gold mini round eyelets with eyelet setter
Black marker (optional)
1/16-inch hole punch
Paper glue
Computer with scanner, printer and matte-finish photo
   paper (optional)

Instructions

Use a computer to generate "Having another birthday?"
and "Don't worry ... 'BIRTHDAYS are good for you.
Statistics show that the people who have the most live
the longest.'"—Larry Lorenzoni, on white card stock,
leaving enough space between quotations for road-
sign photo. *Option: Hand-write quotations on white
card stock with black marker.* Cut a 4½ x 5¾-inch
rectangle around quotations; glue to black card stock.
Trim a small border. Use a computer to print photo on
matte photo paper or use regular photo. Trim photo
to approximately 4 x 2¾ inches. Centre and glue to
layered card stock.

Referring to photo, punch two 1/16-inch holes above and
below photo; set eyelets. Thread elastic cords through
eyelets. Glue assembled panel to card front.

To decorate envelope, use envelope as a template to
trace and cut a piece of red scuffed printed paper to
fit top envelope flap. Adhere paper inside top flap,
applying adhesive to top edge only. This will prevent
paper from crinkling when folded. ■

Having another birthday?

30

Don't worry...

"BIRTHDAYS are good for you.
Statistics show that the people who
have the most **live the longest."**

- LARRY LORENZONI

30 Already?
Printed paper from Karen Foster Design; elastic
cords from 7gypsies.

HYDRANGEA HAPPY BIRTHDAY

Floral photographs and stamps created from moldable foam blocks and dried flowers make it easy to design custom greeting cards.

Design | Judi Kauffman

Materials
Card stock: light green, dark green, light brown
3 (1¾ x 1⅝-inch) hydrangea photos
Pre-dried flowers or a flower press to press your own
Birthday card-stock stickers
Moldable foam stamp blocks
Rainbow dye ink pad
Waxed paper or non-stick sheet
Toothpick or corsage pin
Heat tool
Paper glue

Instructions
Arrange flowers and leaves on a heatproof surface. Following manufacturer's instructions, heat a block of moldable foam and press it against the leaves and flowers on heatproof surface. Use foam block and ink to stamp leaves and flowers on light green and light brown card stock.

Form a 5⅜ x 6½-inch side-fold card from dark green card stock. Cut a 5⅜ x 5½-inch piece of stamped light green card stock; centre and adhere to card front.

Adhere a hydrangea photo to dark green card stock; trim a small border and adhere toward centre top of a 2⅜ x 2¾-inch piece of stamped light brown card stock. Centre and adhere to card front. Referring to photo, adhere remaining two hydrangea photos centred above and below centre photo.

Attach two birthday stickers to dark green card stock; trim small borders and adhere to upper left and lower right areas of card front at an angle. Trim edges even. ■

Hydrangea Happy Birthday
Field, Flower & Stationery Press from Arnold Grummer's; pre-dried flowers from Greetings of Grace, Bloomin' Delights and Nature's Pressed Inc.; card-stock stickers from Karen Foster Design; moldable foam blocks from Clearsnap Inc.; rainbow ink pad from Ranger Industries Inc.; Kid's Choice Glue! from Beacon Adhesives Inc.

BON VOYAGE

*Send wishes for safe travels
to friends and family who are
preparing for an upcoming trip.*

Design | Sharon Reinhart

Materials

Card stock: brown, black, ivory
Ivory envelope to fit a 4½ x 4½-inch card
2 copies (4 x 4-inch) of one sepia-toned photo
Rub-on transfers: "bon voyage," "journey," "trip,"
   "escape," various other travel-themed words
Black marker
3 brown mini round brads
Punches: 1⁄16-inch hole, 1½-inch circle
Adhesive foam tape
Glue stick

Instructions

Form a 4½ x 4½-inch top-fold card from brown card
stock. Adhere one of the photos to black card stock; trim
a narrow border. Punch three 1⁄16-inch holes through lower
left side of photo; insert brads. Apply "bon voyage" rub-on
transfer to upper right corner of photo; apply "journey,"
"trip" and "escape" to lower left corner. Adhere to card
front with foam tape.

Punch a focal point from remaining photo with 1½-inch
circle punch. Use double layers of foam tape to adhere
focal point on matching area on card.

For envelope, cut a 2¾ x 1¾-inch rectangle from ivory
card stock; edge rectangle with black marker. Adhere to
brown card stock and trim a 1⁄8-inch border. Centre and
adhere to envelope front. Apply desired rub-on transfers
to envelope. ■

Bon Voyage
Rub-on transfers from Royal & Langnickel.

BABY GIRL

A close-up photo of a sweet baby face is the ideal way to embellish this simple greeting card.

Design | Tanis Giesbrecht

Materials

Card stock: sage green, brown
Pink floral printed paper
White vellum
Approximately 4 x 3¾-inch baby photo
White envelope to fit a 4¼ x 5½-inch card
Pewter flower brad
White mini tag
Black fine-tip marker (optional)
Alphabet rub-on transfers (optional)
Ribbons: 4¼ inches ⅜-inch-wide sage green grosgrain,
    15¼ inches ½-inch-wide pink-edged organdy,
    4¼ inches ¼-inch-wide brown grosgrain
1/16-inch hole punch
Stapler with staples
Sewing machine with white thread
Removable adhesive
Paper glue
Computer and printer

Instructions

Form a 4¼ x 5½-inch side-fold card from sage green card stock. Adhere a 4¼ x 4⅛-inch piece of pink floral printed paper to top of card front.

Use a computer to generate "baby girl" vertically on printer paper; attach baby photo on top of printed words with removable adhesive, positioning words along left side of photo. Run through printer again; let ink dry completely. *Option: Use alphabet rub-on transfers instead.* Adhere photo to brown card stock; trim a small border. Machine-stitch along photo edges; centre and adhere to card as shown.

Referring to photo, adhere a 4¼-inch length of each ribbon to bottom of card; machine-stitch along centre of each. Use a computer to generate, or hand-print, "Sweet" on mini tag. *Note: If using a computer, follow previous instructions.* Attach tag to lower right corner of card with brad.

Use a computer to generate, or hand-print, birth announcement information on vellum. Cut a rectangle around words and adhere to pink floral printed paper; cut a small border and adhere to brown card stock. Trim a small border; adhere to inside right panel.

For envelope, hand-print, or use a computer to generate, "baby girl" on lower right side of envelope. *Note: If using a computer, follow previous instructions.* Cut a ¾ x 4¼-inch piece of sage green card stock; ink edges. Tie a bow near one end of remaining 11-inch pink ribbon; wrap ribbon vertically around strip, adhering ends to reverse side. Staple ribbon ends at top and bottom of strip; adhere strip to left side of envelope. ■

Inside detail shown above.

Autumn Ava
March 10, 2006
6 lbs 13 oz
19 inches

baby girl

Sweet

baby girl

Baby Girl
Flower brad from Making Memories.

BABY WELCOME

Turn photos of your new bundle of joy into adorable baby announcements with computer and digital image software.

Design | Jacqueline Jones

Materials

White 6¼ x 5-inch top-fold card
Digital photos on computer
Photo paper
Card stock: white, blue
Printed papers: blue/green polka dot, striped, plaid, gingham checked
White mini brads
Decorative-edge scissors
Decorative punches: tag, teddy bear
1⁄16-inch hole punch
Adhesive foam dot
Glue stick
Digital imaging software
Computer and printer

Instructions

Use computer program to crop photos to approximately 4⅜ x 2 inches and soften edges. Above photos, create rectangles and fill with blue. Add "welcome"; fill text with white. Superimpose baby's name over top edge of photos; fill text with blue.

Print photos with "welcome" panels on desired photo paper leaving 1⁄16-inch white border all around.

Option: Crop existing photos; mount on blue card stock to create the colour-block effect. Transfer "welcome" and name with blue and white alphabet rub-on transfers or rubber stamps.

Continuing with instructions for individual card, mount photo on white card stock with glue stick. Tear card-stock edges around photo.

Cut two pieces of complementary printed paper 5⅞ x 2½ inches; adhere to front of card, overlapping edges and leaving narrow border all around.

Cut narrow blue card-stock strip with decorative-edge scissors; adhere across card over seam between printed papers. Adhere photo to card front at an angle.

Punch matching teddy bear shapes from blue card stock and white card stock; punch matching tag shapes from printed paper and white card stock. Adhere matching shapes together with glue stick, offsetting them slightly.

Adhere teddy bear to tag. Punch 1⁄16-inch hole in top of tag; mount white mini brad in hole. Adhere tag to front of card with dimensional adhesive foam dot. ■

Baby Welcome
Digital imaging software from Microsoft.

PRECIOUS

Create this stylish card in either pink or blue to share the news of your new baby girl or boy.

Design | Deanna Hutchison

Materials

Card stock: yellow, pink
Pink/yellow printed papers: plaid, coordinating print
Coordinating printed tag
Baby-themed photo image
Baby-themed words rub-on transfers
½-inch-wide pink with white polka dots sheer ribbon
Fine-tip pen
6 gold round brads
2 gold photo turns with brads
1/16-inch hole punch
Die-cutting machine with A7 Note Card Centre Foldout
   #3 die (#NC602C)
Adhesive foam tape
Paper adhesive
Computer and printer (optional)

Instructions

Form a 5¾ x 3¼-inch top-fold card from yellow card stock. Adhere a 5⅜ x 3-inch piece of plaid printed paper to pink card stock; trim a small border. Attach brads to corners.

Wrap straight end of tag around left side of rectangle and adhere end to reverse side, leaving remainder of tag to flap open on front. Loop ribbon through tag hole; trim ribbon ends at an angle.

Referring to photo, attach photo turns to rectangle, positioning them so they will keep tag closed. Adhere assembled rectangle to card front.

Apply a rub-on transfer to bottom of photo; cut pieces of pink card stock and plaid printed paper to layer behind photo; adhere pieces behind photo. Attach brads to left corners of photo. Adhere photo to tag with foam tape.

Hand-print, or use a computer to generate, birth announcement information on printed paper; cut a rectangle around text to fit behind tag. Adhere to yellow card stock; trim a small border and adhere to card front behind tag.

For envelope, die-cut a note card from yellow card stock. To use as an envelope, fold on crease lines and adhere sides on one panel only. Decorate as desired. ■

Inside detail shown above.

Precious

Printed papers and tag from Daisy D's Paper Co.; photo image from Pebbles Inc.; rub-on transfers from Memories Complete; die-cutting machine and die from AccuCut.

LOVELY BABY GIRL

A sweet photo and a simple design make this card the ideal way to announce the arrival of a precious new baby.

Design | Tami Mayberry

Materials

Card stock: pink, light green
White with baby-themed words printed paper
Pink envelope to fit a 7 x 5-inch card
3 x 3¾-inch baby photo
"It's a girl!" rubber stamp
Ink pads: light brown distress, black dye
"baby girl" rub-on transfer
2 paper flowers: medium, small
Pink mini safety pin
Pink mini round brad
Circle punches: ⅟₁₆-inch, 1¼-inch
Paper glue

Instructions

Form a 7 x 5-inch top-fold card from pink card stock. Cut a 6½ x 4½-inch piece of light green card stock and a 6½ x 3½-inch piece of baby-themed words printed paper; tear off bottom edges of each. Lining up top edges, adhere papers together. Layer two paper flowers and place on lower right portion of layered papers; punch a ⅟₁₆-inch hole through flower centres and insert brad. Adhere assembled piece to card front.

Transfer "baby girl" to lower right corner of card. Adhere photo to a 3½ x 4½-inch piece of light green card stock; ink edges with light brown ink. Attach safety pin to top of layered photo; adhere to left side of card.

For envelope, use top envelope flap as a template to trace and cut a piece of baby-themed words printed paper to fit; adhere paper to envelope flap. Punch a 1¼-inch circle from pink card stock; use black ink to stamp "It's a girl!" on circle. Adhere to top envelope flap. ■

Lovely Baby Girl
Printed paper from Pressed Petals; rubber stamp from Provo Craft; rub-on transfer from The C-Thru Ruler Co.; distress ink pad from Ranger Industries Inc.

WEDDING BOUQUET

Combine digital photos and tea bag folding technique to create the focal point on this stunning card.

Design | Mary Ayres

Materials

Card stock: white, pale pink, pink
Pink envelope to fit a 5 x 7-inch card
8 wallet-size colour copies of rose photo
5 silver round brads
Small and medium metal-edge vellum rectangle tags
Wedding sentiment rub-on transfers
Pink ink pad
1/16-inch hole punch
Sewing machine with silver thread
Paper glue

Instructions

Form a 5 x 7-inch side-fold card from pale pink card stock. Adhere a 3½-inch pink square to the centre of a 4½-inch white square; glue to top of card. Machine-sew a straight stitch around edges of both squares.

Determine what portion of rose photo will be featured for the folding design; cut a 1½-inch square from that same portion of each colour copy. Fold each square in half diagonally with right side of photo face up; score line. Referring to photo for design, unfold squares and fold sides to scored centre line, forming a point at bottom.

Ink edges of each folded photo. Determine and mark centre of pink square on card. Arrange and adhere folded photos symmetrically around centre dot. Punch a 1/16-inch hole in centre of folded design; attach brad.

Transfer wedding sentiment onto medium vellum tag; position tag below folded design. Punch 1/16-inch holes on sides of tag; attach brads.

To embellish envelope, transfer wedding sentiment onto small vellum tag; position on envelope flap. Punch 1/16-inch hole on sides of tag; attach brads. ■

Wedding Bouquet
Rub-on transfers from Royal & Langnickel; Zip
Dry Paper Glue from Beacon Adhesives Inc.

POCKET OF LOVE

Add your own special photo and embellishments to make this pocket card for your valentine.

Design | Madeline Fox

Materials

Deep red library pocket with window
Deep red card stock
Cream/red flower printed paper
Coordinating valentine image
Scrap piece burgundy corrugated paper
Cream round dimensional alphabet letters
"Be Mine" rub-on transfer
Gold ribbon slide
Red and burgundy fibres
2 (⅜–⅝-inch-wide) red or burgundy ribbons
Brown pigment ink pad
Red fabric
Fabric stiffener
Gold star eyelet with eyelet-setting tool
³⁄₁₆-inch hole punch
Glue stick
Project note: Before beginning, treat fabric with fabric stiffener and let dry.

Instructions

Cut a 3½ x 2¼-inch piece of cream floral printed paper; tear off top edge and adhere to bottom edge of library pocket. Ink pocket edges. Cut valentine image slightly larger than window opening; adhere inside opening.

Use pattern on page 44 to trace and cut a large heart from red fabric; adhere heart to lower left side of pocket.

Adhere letters to spell "love" beside heart. Wrap a piece of ribbon around top edge of pocket; tie a knot on left side and trim ribbon ends.

Thread another piece of ribbon through ribbon slide; place ribbon slide on lower left corner of pocket, and wrap and adhere ribbon ends to reverse side.

Cut a 3¼ x 5¼-inch rectangle from deep red card stock; round corners of rectangle, forming a tag. Ink edges. Adhere a ⅝ x ⅝-inch square piece of corrugated paper to centre top of tag; punch a ³⁄₁₆-inch hole through square. Set star eyelet. Thread fibres through eyelet; trim fibre ends. Insert tag into pocket.

For envelope, enlarge pattern on page 44. Use pattern to trace and cut an envelope from red card stock; score and fold on dashed lines. Adhere flaps together. Cut a 4 x 2¼-inch piece of cream floral printed paper; adhere to bottom portion of top envelope flap; trim edges even. Ink edges.

Cut a 4-inch length of ribbon; adhere to top edge of floral printed paper on envelope flap. Use pattern on page 44 to trace and cut a small heart from red fabric; adhere to left side of envelope flap. ■

Pocket of Love
Library pocket from Kopp Design;
ribbon slide from Maya Road.

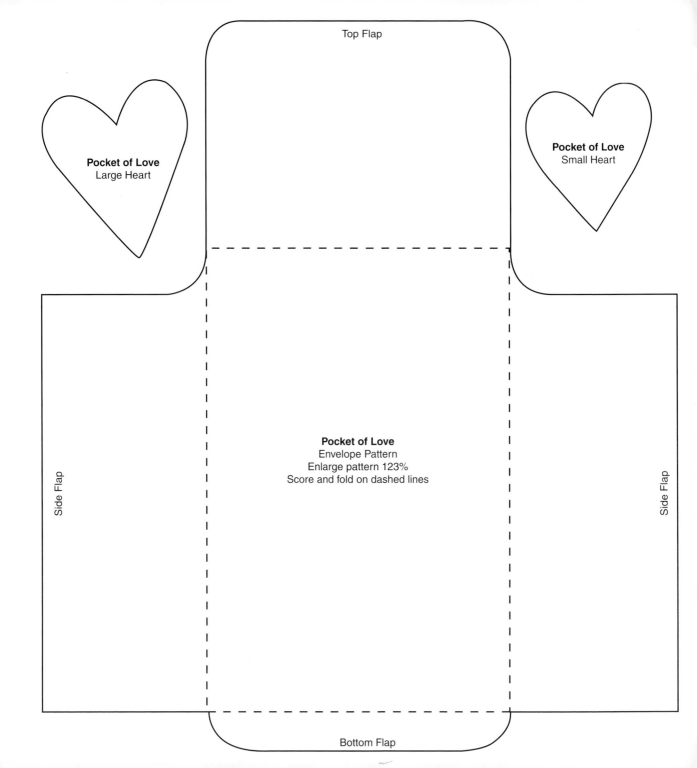

Top Flap

Pocket of Love
Large Heart

Pocket of Love
Small Heart

Side Flap

Side Flap

Pocket of Love
Envelope Pattern
Enlarge pattern 123%
Score and fold on dashed lines

Bottom Flap

LOVE OF MY LIFE

Create this quick and easy card with rub-on transfer sentiments and a romantic photo.

Design | Mary Ayres

Materials

Heavyweight printed papers: turquoise distressed, pink with green polka dots
White envelope to fit a 7 x 5-inch card
2 x 3-inch black-and-white photo
Rub-on transfers: "Love," "love of my life"
3 coordinating fibres
Decorative silver buckle
6 silver mini round brads
1⁄16-inch hole punch
Paper glue

Instructions

Form a 7 x 5-inch top-fold card from turquoise distressed paper. Using pattern on page 47, trace and tear a heart from pink polka-dot print paper. Adhere photo to heart at an angle. Wrap fibres around heart and slide fibre ends through silver buckle, positioning buckle on right side of heart. Adhere heart and buckle to left side of card.

Punch a 1⁄16-inch hole through each corner of photo; insert brads. Cut tail off of "e" on "Love" transfer; rub-on remaining portion of word to lower right corner of card. Transfer "e" tail to upper left corner of card.

Love of My Life
Printed papers from BasicGrey; buckle from Nunn
Design; rub-on transfers from The C-Thru Ruler Co.;
Zip Dry Paper Glue from Beacon Adhesives Inc.

For envelope, cut a 1¾-inch-wide strip of turquoise distressed print paper long enough to fit top envelope flap; glue to envelope flap, trimming ends even with envelope. Tear a 1-inch-wide strip of pink polka-dot print paper the same length; glue to turquoise strip to envelope flap. Trim ends even.

Transfer "love of my life" to centre of pink polka-dot paper on flap; punch a ¹⁄₁₆-inch hole through both ends of strip. Insert brads. ■

Love of My Life
Heart Pattern

EASTER TULIPS

A bucketful of blossoms creates the ideal focal point on this Easter greeting card.

Design | Kathleen Paneitz

Materials

Printed papers: light green, pink/green argyle
3⅛ x 4-inch tulip photo
"Happy Easter" sticker
Tulip jumbo clip
12 inches ½-inch-wide yellow grosgrain ribbon
Sandpaper
Envelope template to fit a 3½ x 5½-inch card
Paper glue

Instructions

Form a 3½ x 5½-inch top-fold card from light green paper. Adhere photo to top right side of card front; attach "Happy Easter" sticker to bottom right side of card. Wrap ribbon around bottom of card front and tie a knot on left side; trim ribbon ends. Attach clip to card so it frames "Happy Easter"; secure clip with glue.

Use envelope template to cut an envelope from argyle printed paper; assemble envelope. Sand edges. ■

Easter Tulips

Light green printed paper from Dream Street Papers; pink/green argyle printed paper, sticker and ribbon from Making Memories; clip from Adornit/Carolee's Creations; envelope template from The C-Thru Ruler Co./Déjà Views; Zip Dry Paper Glue from Beacon Adhesives Inc.

DECORATING EGGS

Strips of torn paper and rub-on transfers make quick work of creating this fun photo card.

Design | Mary Ayres

Materials
Card stock: white, pastel shades of yellow, blue, pink, green, orange, lavender
Green envelope to fit a 5 x 7-inch card
2½ x 3¼-inch Easter photo
Easter sentiments rub-on transfers
Purple dye ink pad
Paper glue

Instructions
Form a 5 x 7-inch side-fold card from white card stock. Tear random-size strips of pastel shades of card stock; adhere strips to card front horizontally, leaving some white space showing. Trim and ink edges.

Adhere photo to lavender card stock; trim a narrow border. Ink edges; adhere to left side of card front as shown. Apply rub-on transfers to card-stock strips.

Decorate envelope as desired. ■

Decorating Eggs
Rub-on transfers from Royal & Langnickel; Zip Dry Paper Glue from Beacon Adhesives Inc.

CHERISHED MEMORIES

In appreciation for a lifetime of love, present your mother with an accordion-style card filled with memories of happy moments.

Design | Linda Beeson

Materials

Card stock: white, pink textured
Printed paper
Small vintage photos
Assorted vintage stickers
Alphabet rubber stamps
Black ink pad
Chalk ink pads: green, pale peach
Brown distress ink pad
Alphabet rub-on transfers
Tiny green buttons
¾-inch safety pin
Decorative brad
Antique photo turn
Black photo corners
Mini snap
Tiny green alphabet beads
Oval "mom" page pebble
Ribbons: pink, green
Flower punches: 1-inch, ⅝-inch
Circle punches: ⅛-inch, 1¼-inch
Decorative-edge scissors
Stapler and green staples
Paper glue
Craft cement
Computer and printer (optional)

Instructions

Accordion-fold a 12 x 4-inch strip of printed paper into four sections. Rub edges with green chalk ink pad.

Panel 1: Hand-print, or use a computer to generate, "thanks for the memories" on white card stock; cut into strips and rub with peach chalk ink pad. Adhere to panel. Centre tiny green buttons over three ⅝-inch flowers punched from pink card stock; adhere over ends of card-stock strips. Staple ribbon over top left edge; use rub-on transfers and/or alphabet stamps to stamp "Mom" under strips.

Panel 2: Rub edges of photo with distress ink. Affix photo corners; adhere to panel. Add stickers, rub-on transfers, and "mom" page pebble.

Panel 3: Knot ribbon onto tiny safety pin; affix to corner of photo. Punch 1-inch flower from pink card stock; set flower aside for Panel 4. Centre punched negative image within punched 1½-inch circle; overlap with photo and adhere to panel. Stamp words using green chalk ink pad. Add other words and embellishments as desired.

Panel 4: Affix punched flower to panel using decorative brad. Adhere photo to panel, overlapping with antique photo turn. Stamp words using green chalk ink pad. Glue tiny alphabet beads to spell "MOM" below photo. Staple ribbon over bottom right edge of panel. ■

Cherished Memories

Printed paper from Autumn Leaves; rubber stamps from Hero Arts; buttons, safety pin, photo turn, mini snap and page pebble from Making Memories; stickers from Bo-Bunny Press; chalk ink pads from Clearsnap.

ENJOY EACH MOMENT

Personalize this quick and easy greeting card with a photo that reflects the simple joys of life.

Design | Kathleen Paneitz

Materials

Card stock: white, dark brown textured
Cork paper
Matte laminate sheet
Rub-on transfers: alphabet, life sentiment
Sheer black ribbon
Colour copy of a black-and-white duck photo
Spoon
Water
Shallow bowl
Spray adhesive

Project note: *Even though it is a black-and-white photo, a colour copy must be used to transfer image well.*

Instructions

Form a 5½ x 4¼-inch top-fold card from brown card stock. Cut a piece of laminate slightly larger than photo; peel backing from laminate sheet and lay it flat, sticky side up, on a smooth surface. Trim colour copy of photo as desired. Press copy onto laminate, image side down. Burnish back of photo with the back of a spoon to make sure image is adhered to laminate.

Fill a shallow bowl with warm water; put laminate with photocopy into water and let soak for five minutes. Take image out of water and carefully begin to peel off paper copy at one corner. Peel as much of the paper off as possible being careful to not rub so hard as to rub image off laminate; let dry.

Spray adhesive on back of image and adhere to white card stock; tear card stock around photo. Adhere photo to cork paper and trim cork paper as desired. Attach to front of card.

Using alphabet rub-ons, transfer the word "Dad" to photo. Transfer the sentiment "enjoy each moment" above photo. Tie ribbon into a bow; adhere below photo. ∎

enjoy each moment

Dad

Enjoy Each Moment
Rub-on transfers from Making Memories;
cork paper from Magenta; laminate sheet
from Xyron; spray adhesive from 3M.

TRICK OR TREAT

*Use photo-editing software to give
your photos a watercolour effect
and a bit of personality!*

Design | Linda Beeson

Materials

Card stock: olive green, black, brown, light brown
Printed papers: green/striped double-sided, brown tweed
Black envelope to fit a 5⅝ x 5⅝-inch card
Digital pumpkin image
3 x 2⅜-inch pumpkin patch photo
Stickers: leaf, pumpkin, felt letters to spell "boo"
Black rub-on transfers: zigzag stitches, "tricK or TrEat"
Twine
Sewing machine with dark brown thread
Paper glue
Computer, printer, photo paper and photo-editing
   software

Instructions

Use photo-editing software to give pumpkin image
a watercolour effect and to add a face on pumpkin.
Print out photo so it measures approximately
4¼ x 3¾ inches.

Form a 5⅝ x 5⅝-inch top-fold card from black card
stock. Centre and adhere a 5¼ x 5¼-inch piece of
double-sided printed paper to card front, green side
face up; adhere a 2⅜ x 5¼-inch piece of double-sided
printed paper to card front ⅜ inch from left edge of card
front, striped side face up. Machine-sew zigzag stitches
along edges of papers next to black card stock.

Adhere pumpkin photo to brown card stock; trim a
narrow border. Adhere to olive green card stock; trim a
small border. Adhere to card front as shown. Apply
"tricK or TrEat" rub-on transfer to lower right corner of
card front. Wrap twine around card front and tie a knot
at top; trim excess twine.

For inside, adhere pumpkin patch photo to light brown
card stock; trim a narrow border. Adhere to olive green
card stock; trim a small border. Adhere inside card. Attach
"boo" stickers to bottom of photo.

Adhere a 2⅛ x 6⅜-inch piece of brown tweed paper to
left side of envelope front; apply zigzag stitches rub-on
transfers along sides of paper. Attach leaf and pumpkin
stickers to bottom of paper strip. ∎

Trick or Treat

Double-sided printed paper from Cosmo Cricket; brown tweed printed paper from The Paper Loft; rub-on sentiment from Making Memories; rub-on stitches from Die Cuts With A View; felt stickers from American Crafts Inc.; leaf and pumpkin stickers from EK Success.

GIVING THANKS

Partner an autumn leaves photo with lovely patterned paper to create this thoughtful greeting card.

Design | Linda Beeson

Materials

Card stock: dark brown/dark red double-sided, brown
Double-sided printed paper
2⅞ x 3⅞-inch leaf photo
Brown dye ink pad
12 inches ½-inch-wide brown striped sheer ribbon
Black epoxy letter stickers
Sewing machine with brown thread
Decorative-edge scissors
Craft knife
Paper glue

Instructions

Form a 3¾ x 7¼-inch side-fold card from double-sided card stock with the dark brown side as the outside. Cut a 3½ x 7-inch piece of printed paper; ink edges and adhere to card front; machine-sew a zigzag stitch along edges of paper.

Adhere photo to reverse side of printed paper; trim a small border. Adhere to brown card stock and trim a small border with decorative-edge scissors. Adhere to card as shown. Machine-sew a straight stitch along edges of printed paper around photo. Attach stickers below photo to spell "giving Thanks."

Open card and use craft knife to cut a ½-inch slit along fold 2¼ inches from bottom; thread ribbon through slit and knot on front. Trim ribbon ends. ■

Giving Thanks

Card stock from WorldWin Papers; printed paper from Cosmo Cricket; stickers from Creative Imaginations.

SNOWY ARBOUR

A snow-covered scene makes the ideal photo to include on a simple Christmas card.

Design | Kathleen Paneitz

Materials

Card stock: dark green, black, white

Double-sided striped printed paper

4 x 3-inch winter photo

12 inches ⅜-inch-wide white "Peace on Earth" satin ribbon

"Merry Christmas" mini card-stock tag

White safety pin

Envelope template to fit a 5¾ x 3⅝-inch card

Corner rounder

Paper glue

Instructions

Form a 5¾ x 3⅝-inch side-fold card from dark green card stock; round corners. Cut a 5½ x 3¼-inch rectangle from black card stock; round corners. Wrap ribbon around left side of rectangle and knot; trim ribbon ends at an angle. Adhere assembled rectangle to card front.

Adhere photo to white card stock; trim a small border and adhere to card as shown. Use safety pin to attach "Merry Christmas" tag to ribbon knot.

Use envelope template to cut an envelope from printed paper; assemble envelope. ■

Snowy Arbour

Printed paper from My Mind's Eye; ribbon from
American Crafts Inc.; tag and safety pin from Making
Memories; envelope template from The C-Thru Ruler
Co.; Zip Dry Paper Glue from Beacon Adhesives Inc.

JINGLE ALL THE WAY

This fun photo and matching embellishments combine for a perfect Christmas greeting and gift card.

Design | Linda Valentino

Materials
White card stock
Gold paper
Digital images of jingle bells
Jingle bells: 1 (⅜-inch) silver, 2 (¼-inch) gold
Metallic cord: 15 inches gold, 22 inches silver
Metallic ribbon: 3 inches ⅜-inch-wide silver with gold
   edging, 15 inches ⅛-inch-wide silver
Black fine-tip marker (optional)
Size 7 brass snap swivel
Craft knife
Tape
Paper glue
Computer, printer and photo paper

Instructions
Use digital images to print two photos, one measuring 2½ x 2½ inches and the other measuring 5 x 3½ inches.

For mini card, form a 3⅜ x 3½-inch top-fold card from white card stock. On card front only, use craft knife to cut two ⅜-inch vertical slits ¼ inch apart at centre and about ¼ inch from top fold. Insert ends of ⅜-inch-wide ribbon through slits from front to back; cross ends over each other inside and insert ends through opposite slits from back to front. Trim ribbon ends in V-notches. Adhere

2½ x 2½-inch photo to gold paper; trim a small border. Centre and adhere to card front.

For larger card, form a 5½ x 5½-inch top-fold card from white card stock. Slide bells on snap swivel; close securely. Tie a 7-inch length of silver cord onto top of swivel. Wrap this cord, along with remaining ribbon and cords, around left side of larger photo; tape ends to back. Adhere photo to gold paper; trim a small border; centre and adhere to top of card front.

Use a computer to generate, or hand-print, "Jingle all the way" on white card stock. Cut a 3 x ¾-inch rectangle around words; adhere to gold paper; trim a small border. Centre and adhere below photo.

For inside, on white card stock, use a computer to generate, or hand-print:

Christmas is a time of joy,
A time for love and cheer,
A time for making memories
To last throughout the year.

Cut a rectangle around sentiment; adhere to gold paper. Trim a small border; adhere inside card. ■

Christmas is a time of joy,
A time for love and cheer,
A time for making memories
To last throughout the year.

Inside detail shown above.

Jingle all the way

Jingle All The Way
Zip Dry Paper Glue from
Beacon Adhesives Inc.

DAFFODIL DREAMS

Use photos from your garden to create a one-of-a-kind springtime card.

Design | Kathleen Paneitz

Materials
Card stock: light green, cream rib-textured
White with springtime-themed words printed paper
Colour copy of daffodil photo
Matte-finish laminate sheet
Embossed and glittered daffodil stickers
Light green dye ink pad
7⁄16-inch-wide yellow polka-dot sheer ribbon
Envelope template to fit a 6¼ x 4⅜-inch card
Shallow bowl filled with warm water
Spray adhesive
Glue stick

Instructions
Form a 6¼ x 4⅜-inch top-fold card from light green card stock. Centre and adhere a 6¼ x 4-inch piece of springtime-themed words printed paper to card front.

Cut a piece of laminate slightly larger than daffodil photo; peel off backing from laminate and lay it flat, sticky side up, on work surface. Trim colour copy of photo as desired and press onto laminate with image side down; burnish back of photo to ensure that it is adhered securely.

Place laminate-covered photo into warm water; let soak for five minutes. Take photo out, and beginning at one corner, carefully peel off paper copy leaving photo image on laminate. Let dry. Trim laminate as needed; spray adhesive on back of image and adhere to card front.

Attach daffodil sticker to cream rib-textured card stock; trim around sticker as desired and ink edges. Adhere to upper right corner of card. Tie a knot with ribbon; adhere to sticker.

Use envelope template to trace and cut an envelope from light green card stock; score and fold to form envelope flaps. Adhere side and bottom flaps together. Attach a daffodil sticker to cream rib-textured card stock; trim around sticker as desired and ink edges. Adhere to left side of envelope. ■

Daffodil Dreams
Printed paper from The Crafter's Workshop;
stickers from K&Company; laminate sheet from
Xyron; template from The C-Thru Ruler Co.

SPRING GREETINGS

A photo printed on vellum paper creates a soft focal point on this spring greeting card.

Design | Karen Robinson

Materials

Card stock: green, white, beige
White vellum
Digital photo of a bunny or bunny photo
   from a magazine
Envelope to fit a 7 x 5¾-inch card
Green twill ribbon
Silk flower
Brown chalk
3 gold mini round brads
Punches: ¹⁄₁₆-inch hole, triangle corner
Sewing machine with beige all-purpose thread
Repositionable adhesive
Glue stick
Computer and printer

Instructions

If using a computer, set image size to 5 x 3 inches and print on vellum; cut out image, leaving a ¼-inch border. *Option: Instead of printing a digital image on vellum, use a photo or image cut from a magazine.* Cut a 6 x 3⅞-inch piece of white card stock; chalk edges. Machine-sew photo to card stock. Tear and crumple edges of bunny image.

Form a 7 x 5¾-inch top-fold card from green card stock. Punch two triangle corners from beige card stock; adhere layered photo to top portion of card, placing a triangle underneath lower right and upper left corners of photo before adhering. Punch a ¹⁄₁₆-inch hole through same corners; insert brads.

Cut a 7 x ⅞-inch strip of white card stock; chalk edges. Using a zigzag stitch, machine-sew to bottom portion of card front.

Use a computer to generate "Springtime Greetings" on computer paper, leaving 1¼ inches between words. Using repositionable adhesive, adhere a 7-inch length of twill ribbon on top of printed sentiment. Run through printer again to print sentiment on twill. Remove twill ribbon from paper; fray edges and adhere to card stock on card. *Option: Hand-write sentiment on twill.* Place flower between words; punch a ¹⁄₁₆-inch hole through flower centre and insert brad.

For envelope, alter size of digital photo to approximately 3 x 1¾ inches; print on computer paper. Repeat to make another image approximately 2½ x 1⅜ inches. *Option: Use magazine photos.* Carefully disassemble envelope by gently separating side and bottom flaps. Using a zigzag stitch, machine-sew smallest photo to top envelope flap; repeat to machine-sew remaining photo to lower left corner on envelope front. Reassemble envelope. ■

Springtime Greetings

Spring Greetings
Corner punch from EK Success.

SPRING FLOWERS

Nothing says "Welcome Spring" better than a bouquet of bright pastel blossoms.

Design | Kathleen Paneitz

Materials
Card stock: white, pale green
Coordinating printed papers: burnt orange with pale green polka dots, cream floral, burnt orange with flower-themed words
3½ x 3⅛-inch "spring" cutout
2⅝ x 2⅞-inch flower photo
"all for you" rub-on transfer
³⁄₁₆-inch-wide green striped ribbon
Nickel photo turn
Orange brad
Envelope template to fit a 6 x 4½-inch card
Sandpaper
⅛-inch hole punch
Mini adhesive dot
Glue stick

Project note: Sand edges of each piece before adhering.

Instructions
Form a 6 x 4½-inch top-fold card from white card stock. Cut a 6 x 4½-inch piece of burnt orange polka-dot printed paper; adhere a 3 x 1⅜-inch piece of pale green card stock to lower right portion of burnt orange piece. Cut a 3⅛ x 4⅛-inch piece of cream floral printed paper; adhere to left side of burnt orange piece. Adhere "spring" cutout to right side of same piece, overlapping other papers. Cut a rectangle around "flowers" from flower-themed word printed paper and adhere to cream floral printed paper; trim a narrow border and adhere to bottom portion of cutout.

Adhere photo to pale green card stock; trim a narrow border and adhere to left side of burnt orange piece. Transfer "all for you" to upper left corner above photo. Tie a bow with ribbon and use mini adhesive dot to adhere it to top of cutout. Punch a ⅛-inch hole through pale green card stock on lower right portion of paper; attach photo turn with orange brad. Adhere assembled piece to card front.

For envelope, use template to trace and cut an envelope from cream floral printed paper; score and fold to form envelope flaps. Adhere side and bottom flaps together. ∎

Spring Flowers

Printed papers from My Mind's Eye; rub-on transfer and brad from Making Memories; photo turn from 7gypsies; template from The C-Thru Ruler Co.

SUMMER ESCAPE

*Share good wishes for a relaxing summer
day with a simple photo greeting card.*

Design | Kathleen Paneitz

Materials
Card stock: white, blue textured, light brown
Vacation-themed stickers
"relax" definition
Metal feet plaque
"leave it all behind" rub-on transfer
Sandals in the sand photo
Antique white acrylic paint
Sandpaper
Envelope template to fit a 6⅛ x 4⅝-inch card
Foam paintbrush
³⁄₁₆-inch-wide double-sided tape
Glue stick

Instructions
Form a 6⅛ x 4⅝-inch top-fold card from white card stock.
Glue a 6⅛ x 4⅝-inch piece of blue card stock to card
front.

Trim photo to a 4⅜ x 3¼-inch rectangle; layer onto white
card stock, trimming a small border. Glue in upper left
corner of card. Attach a vacation-themed sticker in lower
right corner of card. Glue "relax" definition in lower left
corner, overlapping corner of photo. Transfer "leave it all
behind" below definition.

Use foam paintbrush to apply a very light coat of antique
white paint onto metal plaque. Let dry and adhere plaque
in upper right corner of card using double-sided tape.

For envelope, use template to trace and cut an envelope
from light brown card stock. Score and fold envelope
flaps; adhere side and bottom flaps together. Lightly sand
all edges. Attach vacation-themed stickers in lower left
corner on front of envelope. ■

relax (ri·laks) 1. to release tension 2. to rest from work 3. to be at ease 4. to release physical or mental pressures from oneself

leave it all behind

ESCAPE:
1. a getaway
2. leave stress and worries behind
3. REFRESH AND RELAX
4. mental release FROM REALITY

VACATION:

take ME Away

Summer Escape

Stickers, definition, metal feet plaque and rub-on transfer from Making Memories; envelope template from The C-Thru Ruler Co.

EASY SUMMERTIME

Send this sweet and yummy greeting card for any summertime occasion.

Design | Kathleen Paneitz

Materials

White card stock
Striped printed paper
5⅝ x 3-inch watermelon photo
Stickers: clear "SUMMERTIME," 2 watermelon slices
Black decorative border rub-on transfers
18 inches ¼-inch-wide green striped ribbon
Envelope template to fit a 5⅝ x 4⅜-inch card
Paper adhesive

Instructions

Form a 5⅝ x 4⅜-inch top-fold card from white card stock. Adhere watermelon photo to card front ⅜ inch from top edge. Wrap and adhere ribbon around card front and tie ends in a bow on front; trim ribbon ends at an angle. Apply decorative border rub-on transfers to top and bottom edges of card. Attach "SUMMERTIME" sticker to lower left side of card.

Use envelope template to cut an envelope from printed paper; assemble envelope. Decorate front of envelope with rub-on transfers and watermelon slice stickers. ■

Easy Summertime

Printed paper from Doodlebug Design Inc.; watermelon slices stickers from Mrs. Grossman's; "SUMMERTIME" sticker from Autumn Leaves; decorative border rub-on transfers from Lasting Impressions for Paper Inc. and KI Memories; envelope template from The C-Thru Ruler Co.

SUMMER SUNSHINE

Send a quick hello with this sunny summertime greeting card.

Design | Linda Valentino

Materials

Card stock: white, turquoise, black
Envelope to fit a 5 x 7-inch card
2 sunflower photos
Black fine-tip marker
Stickers: 2 sunflower borders, 1 single sunflower
Black rub-on transfers: "Summer," "sunshine"
White slide mount
3 yellow flower eyelets and eyelet-setting tool
Corner rounder
⅛-inch hole punch
Paper glue
Adhesive foam squares
Removable tape (optional)
Computer and printer (optional)

Instructions

Form a 5 x 7-inch side-fold card from white card stock. Hand-print, or use a computer to generate, desired sentiment inside card. *Note: If using a computer, first print sentiment on printer paper. Use removable tape to attach card on top of printed words and run through printer again.*

Centre and adhere a 4⅞ x 3¾-inch piece of black card stock to a 4⅞ x 6¾-inch piece of turquoise card stock. Trim one sunflower photo to 3½ x 4¾ inches; round corners. Adhere to white card stock; trim a small border and adhere to turquoise/black rectangle as shown.

Punch three ⅛-inch holes through upper left side of black portion of rectangle; set flower eyelets. Adhere assembled panel to card front. Apply "Summer" rub-on transfer to upper left corner of card.

Cut a sunflower from second photo to fit slide mount; adhere to reverse side so it shows through opening. Apply "sunshine" to left side of slide mount; use foam squares to adhere slide mount to lower right corner of card.

Decorate inside of card and envelope with printed papers and sunflower stickers. ■

Summer Sunshine
Stickers from Frances Meyer Inc.; rub-on transfers from Royal & Langnickel; Zip Dry Paper Glue from Beacon Adhesives Inc.

BEACH SHELLS

There's no better way to send warm summer wishes than this fun beach-themed photo card.

Design | Linda Valentino

Materials
Card stock: white, blue, black, tan
Envelope to fit a 7 x 5-inch card
6 x 4-inch photo of shells
3 small shells
Stickers: 2 shells, 1 sand dollar
Plastic letter tiles to spell "BEACH"
15 inches string
Black fine-tip marker
Paper crimper
Mini adhesive dots
Paper glue
Computer and printer (optional)

Instructions
Form a 7 x 5-inch top-fold card from white card stock. Centre and adhere a 6¾ x 4¾-inch piece of blue card stock to card front. Adhere photo to black card stock; trim a ⅛-inch border. Adhere to card as shown.

Cut a 7½ x 2-inch piece of tan card stock; run through paper crimper. Tear off top and bottom edges. Adhere to bottom of card front; trim ends. Use adhesive dots to adhere letter tiles to crimped strip as shown.

Unravel 1 inch on each end of string; referring to photo, adhere string to crimped strip on card. Use adhesive dots to adhere shells to crimped strip as shown.

Hand-print, or use a computer to generate, "May your time be filled with relaxing sunsets, cool drinks, and sand between your toes." on tan card stock; cut a 6¾ x 4¾-inch rectangle around words and adhere inside card. Attach two shell stickers to lower right corner inside card.

Carefully take apart premade envelope and use as a template to cut an envelope from tan card stock; assemble envelope. Decorate envelope with cut strips of card stock and sand dollar sticker. ■

Inside detail shown above.

Beach Shells
Letter tiles from Westrim Crafts;
stickers from EK Success; Zip Dry
Paper Glue from Beacon Adhesives Inc.

FALL PUMPKINS

Add texture and interest to a simple window card with velvety letter stickers.

Design | Kathleen Paneitz

Materials

5 x 5-inch window card with envelope

Black card stock

Approximately 3¾ x 3½-inch pumpkin photo

Stickers: black velvet letters to spell "FALL," clear autumn-themed quotation

"celebrate" rub-on transfer

Raffia

Paper glue

Instructions

Adhere photo to black card stock; trim a ⅛-inch border. Adhere inside card so pumpkins show through window. Attach velvet letter stickers to bottom of card front to spell "FALL." Apply "celebrate" rub-on transfer to upper left corner of card front. Tie several strands of raffia together in a bow; trim ends and adhere to upper right corner of window. Attach clear quotation sticker to envelope as desired. ■

Fall Pumpkins
Card and envelope from The C-Thru Ruler Co.; sticker from
Creative Imaginations; rub-on transfer and velvet stickers from
Making Memories; Zip Dry Paper Glue from Beacon Adhesives Inc.

FALL COLOURS

Layer digital photos printed on an assortment of paper to create a unique fall greeting card.

Design | Mary Ayres

Materials
Card stock: light brown, brown, black, metallic gold,
   4 shades of yellow/orange
Coordinating envelope to fit a 7 x 5-inch card
White vellum
Computer photo paper
Photo of autumn leaves
Brown ink pad
2 gold mini round brads
1⁄16-inch hole punch
Spray sealer
Paper glue
Computer with scanner, printer and
   photo-editing software

Instructions
Form a 7 x 5-inch top-fold card from brown card stock. Ink edges. Centre and glue a 6½ x 4½-inch piece of black card stock to card front.

Cut a 6¼ x 4¼-inch piece of light brown card stock; ink edges and glue to card. Using pattern, trace and cut two corners from metallic gold card stock; glue metallic gold corners to lower left and upper right corners of light brown rectangle on card, lining up straight edges.

Using computer and scanner, scan leaf photo and print two copies on photo paper; trim each image to

2½ x 3³⁄₁₆ inches. Ink edges; set aside one image to be used later on envelope.

Using computer and photo-editing software, change photo image to black and white. Print black-and-white image on the four varying shades of yellow/orange card stocks. Trim each image to the same size as the first coloured photo image. Referring to photo, overlap and adhere printed images to card, with coloured image on top in lower right corner.

Use a computer to generate, or hand-print, "Beautiful Fall Foliage" on vellum; spray words with sealer to set ink. Tear a 5½ x 1-inch rectangle around words; place rectangle on card, referring to photo for placement. Punch a 1⁄16-inch hole on each end of vellum rectangle; insert brads.

For envelope, cut a 1¼ x 5¾-inch strip of light brown card stock; ink edges. Glue strip to left side of envelope. Glue remaining coloured photo image to black card stock; trim a small border and glue to upper left corner of envelope, overlapping light brown strip. ■

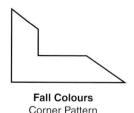

Fall Colours
Corner Pattern

Fall Colours
Spray sealer from Krylon.

FALL HARVEST

The use of multiple prints of one photo adds to the interest of this card design.

Design | Janice Musante

Materials

Orange card stock
Printed papers: orange, brown/green polka dots
White paper
Pale green vellum
White envelope to fit a 5½ x 7⅜-inch card
4 (3 x 2-inch) pumpkin/gourd photos
Black fine-tip marker
Raffia
Pewter oval metal bookplate with brads to fit
10 pewter round brads
¹⁄₁₆-inch hole punch
Paper glue
Computer and printer (optional)

Instructions

Form a 5½ x 7⅜-inch side-fold card from orange card stock. Adhere a 3⅜ x 7¼-inch piece of orange printed paper to centre of card front, aligning bottom edges. Cut two ⅜ x 7⅜-inch strips of polka dots paper; adhere to each side of card front as shown.

Adhere three photos to card front.

Punch a ¹⁄₁₆-inch hole through upper left edge of orange printed paper beside top photo; insert a brad. Repeat to attach a brad to each side of photos. Twist a 4-inch length of raffia around each brad; trim ends.

Hand-print, or use a computer to generate, "Fall Harvest" on vellum; cut an oval around words to fit bookplate; cut an oval from white paper the same size. Place vellum oval on top of white oval and adhere to back of bookplate. Place bookplate on centre bottom of card front; secure with brads.

For inside, adhere a 5 x 6½-inch piece of polka dots paper to left panel inside card to cover brad ends. Hand-print, or use a computer to generate, "Reap the rewards of friendship!" on orange printed paper; cut a 5½ x 1½-inch rectangle around words. Tear off bottom edge and adhere to right panel inside card. Adhere a 5½ x ½-inch strip of polka dots paper to top edge of orange strip.

Decorate envelope as desired. ∎

Fall Harvest
Brown/green polka dots printed paper from K&Company; orange printed paper from Chatterbox Inc.; pale green vellum from ANW Crestwood/The Paper Co.; bookplate and brads from Making Memories; Zip Dry Paper Glue from Beacon Adhesives Inc.

FRESH SNOW

What a refreshing way to display a perfect winter photo—placed on the front of a stamped tag that can hang on a wall or stand on a shelf.

Design | Kathleen Paneitz

Materials

Card stock: grey, tan
Grey distressed printed paper
Desired snow photo, approximately 4 x 2⅜ inches
Large snowflake foam stamp
White acrylic paint
2 silver small binder clips
Snowflake metal charm
"snowed in" paper tag
"sparkle" definition
Rub-on transfers: "fresh," "Snow," "brrr ..."
Silver jump ring
⅞-inch-wide blue/brown ribbon
Sandpaper
Stapler with staples
Foam brush
Circle cutter (optional)
Glue stick

Instructions

Cut a 4⅛ x 5-inch rectangle from grey card stock. Using circle cutter, round top corners of rectangle by only cutting halfway around circle. *Option: Use the edge of a plate or circle template to trace and cut rounded edge.* Sand edges of tag.

Use foam brush to apply white paint to snowflake stamp; stamp snowflake on upper right and lower left portions of tag. Let dry.

Cut a 1½ x 5-inch strip of grey distressed printed paper; sand edges and cut in half. Adhere one half to upper left corner of tag; adhere remaining half to lower right corner. Trim edges even.

Adhere photo to tan card stock; trim a narrow border. Sand edges. Adhere to tag; attach clips to both sides of layered photo. Open jump ring and slide on snowflake charm and "snowed in" tag; attach jump ring to clip on right side of tag; close jump ring. Adhere "sparkle" definition to lower left corner of photo.

Using rub-on transfers, transfer "fresh Snow" to upper left corner of tag on grey distressed printed paper; transfer "brrr ..." on lower right corner on grey distressed printed paper.

Fold a 6-inch length of ribbon in half and staple folded end to centre top edge of tag. Trim ribbon ends. ■

Fresh Snow
Printed paper from BasicGrey; foam stamp from Duncan Enterprises; definition, paper tag, snowflake charm, ribbon and rub-on transfers from Making Memories; clips from Design Originals.

Snowy Morning

Choose your favourite winter-scene photo and use it as the centrepiece of a striking card.

Design | Kathleen Paneitz

Materials

Card stock: white, light brown, light blue
Winter photo
White small alphabet rub-on transfers
1-inch-wide printed twill tape
Metallic blue fibre
Small magnifying glass
White acrylic paint
Snowflake foam stamp
Envelope template to fit a 4¼ x 5⅛-inch card
Circle punches: 1¾-inch, 1¼-inch
Snowflake punch
Paper glaze
Double-sided tape

Instructions

Form a 4¼ x 5⅛-inch top-fold card from white card stock. Cut a 4¼ x 5⅛-inch piece of light brown card stock; use double-sided tape to adhere card stock to card front.

Trim photo to approximately 4 x 5 inches. Punch a 1¾-inch circle from lower right portion of photo.

Cut a piece of light blue card stock large enough to cover circle opening; adhere card stock to reverse side of photo, covering opening. Punch a 1¼-inch circle from light brown card stock; centre and adhere inside circle opening. Punch a snowflake from white card stock; use paper glaze to adhere snowflake to centre of light brown circle.

Adhere assembled photo to card front. Using double-sided tape, adhere twill tape to photo just above circle opening, wrapping and adhering ends inside card. Use rub-ons to transfer "SNOWY AM" to upper right corner of photo.

Tie fibre around handle of magnifying glass; trim ends. Apply paper glaze to rim of magnifying glass and adhere glass to layered snowflake circle. Let dry.

For envelope, use template to trace and cut an envelope from light blue card stock; score and fold to form envelope flaps. Adhere side and bottom flaps together. Use white paint to stamp snowflake in lower left corner on front of envelope; let dry. ∎

On the card:

SNOWY AM

cold ❄ SNOW ANGEL bli... ❄
SNOW FLAKES WHITE WORLD SNOW
playing in the snow ❄ ...flakes... FROST

Snowy Morning
Rub-on transfers from Autumn Leaves; twill tape from
Adornit/Carolee's Creations; magnifying glass from
Manto Fev; template from The C-Thru Ruler Co.; foam
stamp and paper glaze from Duncan Enterprises Inc.

WINTER WONDERLAND

A black-and-white photo reprint creates a stunning focal point on this holiday greeting card.

Design | Karen Robinson

Materials

Card stock: white textured, navy blue
Scrap paper
Silver snowflake charm
Silver jump ring
Silver metallic fibre
2 silver mini brads
Silver metallic acrylic paint
Digital winter tree image (optional)
Photo-transfer pen
White envelope to fit a 5¼-inch square card
Paintbrush
¹⁄₁₆-inch hole punch
Photocopier
Sewing machine with silver thread
Glue stick
Computer and printer
Photo-editing software
Project note: When using a photo-transfer pen, follow manufacturer's instructions and use in a well-ventilated area.

Instructions

Form a 5¼ x 5¼-inch top-fold card from navy blue card stock. Using photo-editing software, change digital image on computer to black and white; create a feathered border around image. Print image onto white textured card stock. *Option: Mat a black-and-white photo of a snow-covered tree onto white textured card stock.* Make a photocopy of image on a toner-based copier, reducing image 25 per cent; set photocopy aside. Trim card stock to approximately 2⅞ x 4¼ inches.

Use a computer to generate, or hand-print, "Winter Wonderland" onto white textured card stock; trim a rectangle around words, allowing room at each end for a brad. Referring to photo for placement, adhere image and word rectangles to card. Punch a ¹⁄₁₆-inch hole at each end of word rectangle; insert brads. Machine-stitch around edges of rectangles.

Paint a rough border of silver metallic around edges of card. Wrap fibre through card and around to front positioning fibre between rectangles; tie a knot to secure. Attach snowflake charm above knot with jump ring.

To embellish envelope, place a piece of scrap paper inside to prevent transfer pen from bleeding through. Place photocopied image face down on lower left corner of envelope. Using even pressure, rub transfer pen on reverse side of photocopy until image is transferred, being careful to not move paper until transfer is complete. ∎

Winter Wonderland

WINTER GREETINGS

Back a winter photo with "snow"-flecked mesh. Icy ribbon adds a wintry touch!

Design | Mary Ayres

Materials

White card stock
Clear vellum
Speckled blue netting
3 x 4½-inch horizontal winter photo
2 (3-inch) pieces ¼-inch-wide sheer iridescent ribbon
2 (⅛-inch) round white eyelets
Winter sentiment rub-on transfer
Light blue ink pad
Craft sponge
Rotary tool and scoring blade
⅛-inch hole punch
Pinking shears
Paper glue

Instructions

Form a 5 x 7-inch top-fold card from white card stock. Use craft sponge to apply blue ink to edges of card. Cut a 4¾ x 6¾-inch rectangle from white card stock; apply blue ink to edges and glue to card. Cut a 5¼ x 3-inch piece of netting; trim bottom edge with pinking shears. Fold the top ½ inch of netting over top of card and glue to secure. Leave remaining netting loose.

Cut two rectangles from white card stock with one measuring 3¼ x 4¾ inches and the other measuring 3½ x 5 inches. Apply blue ink to edges; layer and adhere photo and rectangles. Wrap ribbon diagonally across top right and bottom left corners of layered rectangles, gluing ends on back. Adhere layered rectangle to card, centring rectangle over netting.

Transfer winter sentiment onto vellum; tear a 1½ x 3½-inch rectangle around word and apply blue ink to edges. Place vellum word over bottom right corner of photo; punch a hole on each end of the vellum and attach eyelets to holes. ■

Winter Greetings
Rub-on transfer from Royal & Langnickel; Zip
Dry Paper Glue from Beacon Adhesives Inc.

MAPLE LEAF

While this card showcases a maple leaf, use a leaf from your favourite tree to frame an autumn photo.

Design | Mary Ayres

Materials
Card stock: white, brown, light brown
3½ x 5-inch horizontal photo
2 (⅛-inch) round antique brass eyelets with eyelet setter
Brown dye ink pad
Off-white burlap strand
Craft sponge
⅛-inch hole punch
Rotary tool and scoring blade
Sewing machine with black all-purpose thread
Paper glue
Computer and printer (optional)

Instructions
Form a 4¼ x 5½-inch side-fold card from light brown card stock. Cut a 4 x 5¼-inch rectangle from brown card stock. Using pattern on page 92, cut out maple leaf from brown rectangle. Apply brown ink to inside and outside edges with a craft sponge. Adhere photo on back of rectangle with image centred inside leaf; glue rectangle to card.

Machine-stitch around edge of brown rectangle and around maple leaf following dashed lines on pattern. Hand-print, or use a computer to generate, "maple leaf" on white card stock; cut a ½ x 1¾-inch rectangle around words, leaving extra space on right side. Punch a ⅛-inch hole in right side of rectangle and on right side of stem; attach eyelets. Insert burlap strand through eyelets; knot ends together and trim ends. Glue word rectangle to card. ■

Maple Leaf
Zip Dry Paper Glue from
Beacon Adhesives Inc.

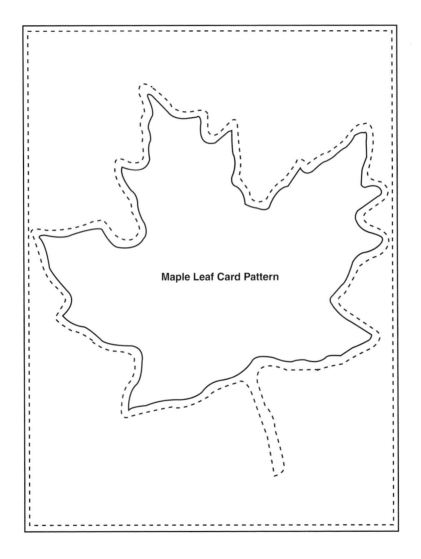

Maple Leaf Card Pattern

VINTAGE THANK YOU

Use vintage photos to create personalized thank you cards.

Design | Kathy Wegner

Materials
Printed card stock
Chipboard photo strip
Slide mounts
Rub-on transfers and/or alphabet beads
Fibres
Distress ink pad, desired colour (optional)
4 photo anchors or 4 eyelets with eyelet-setting tool
Hole punch
Craft knife (optional)
Adhesive foam strips
Paper glue

Instructions
Cut two 3⅞-inch squares from printed card stock. With printed sides faceup, either adhere two photo anchors to the top edge of each square, approximately ½ inch from sides, or set two eyelets, approximately 1⅜ inch apart, on the left edge of each square. If gluing photo anchors, let glue dry before moving to next step. Stack squares on top of each other and tie fibres through photo anchors or eyelets to connect squares; trim fibre ends as needed.

Cut desired photo from chipboard strip and adhere to reverse side of slide mount. *Note: If using a photo smaller than slide-mount opening, cut a piece of printed card stock slightly larger than slide-mount opening and use a craft knife to cut out a rectangle opening, creating a photo mat. Adhere photo to mat then adhere, centred, to slide mount.*

To embellish slide mount, either apply rub-on transfers or slide alphabet beads onto fibres to spell desired words. Wrap fibres around slide mount, securing beads with glue; secure fibre ends on back with glue. Let dry. Adhere assembled slide mount to card using glue or foam strips.

For envelope, use pattern on page 95 to trace and cut an envelope from printed card stock; fold and assemble envelope. ■

Vintage Thank You
Printed card stock, chipboard photo strips and slide mounts
from Design Originals; rub-on transfer from Royal &
Langnickel; Zip Dry Paper Glue from Beacon Adhesives Inc.

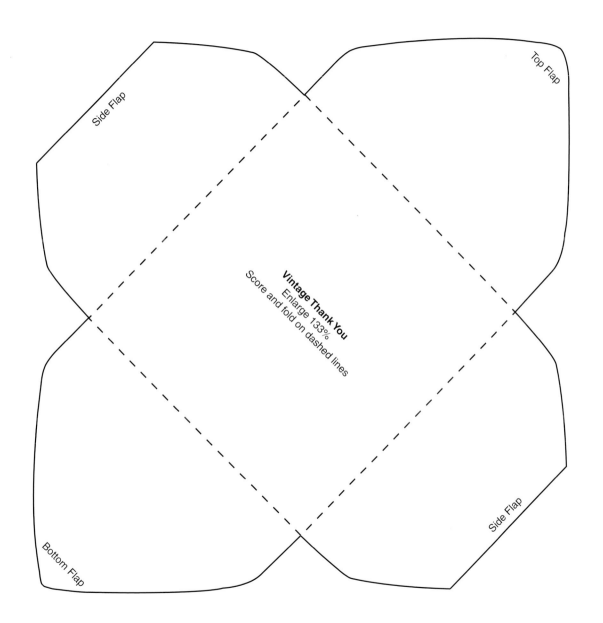

Side Flap

Top Flap

Vintage Thank You
Enlarge 133%
Score and fold on dashed lines

Bottom Flap

Side Flap

LIMITED EDITION

Machine-stitch a photo onto card stock to create a one-of-a-kind greeting card.

Design | Linda Beeson

Materials
White card stock
Printed papers: assorted distressed prints,
    red with green polka dots, green
Brown envelope to fit a 5½ x 5½-inch card
Sepia-tone flower photo
Assorted rub-on transfers
Brown dye ink pad
Sandpaper
Sewing machine with brown thread
Glue stick or double-sided tape
Computer, printer and matte-finish computer paper

Instructions
Form a 5½ x 5½-inch top-fold card from white card stock. Use pattern to trace and cut two large corners from different distressed printed papers; ink edges. Adhere corners to upper left and lower right corners of card front. Ink card edges.

Use computer and printer to print photo on matte-finish paper and trim to approximately 2¾ x 3¼ inches; sand edges. *Option: Use original photo instead of printing it on matte-finish paper.* Adhere photo to green printed paper; trim a ⅛-inch border. Ink edges. Adhere again to red with green polka dots printed paper at an angle; trim desired border and ink edges. Machine-sew a zigzag stitch along edges of green printed paper. Centre

and adhere photo to card front. Apply desired rub-on transfers to card.

Cut a piece of distressed printed paper to fit top envelope flap; ink edges and adhere paper to flap. Use pattern to trace and cut two small corners from distressed printed paper; ink edges and adhere to bottom corners of top envelope flap. Apply desired rub-on transfers to left side of flap. ■

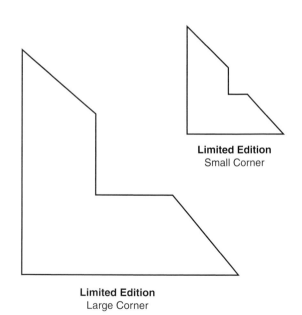

Limited Edition
Small Corner

Limited Edition
Large Corner

THE JOY OF DISCOVERY

delight

DREAM
HEART'S DESIRE

LIMITED EDITION
1 of 50

'05 '05 '05
CERTIFIED

Limited Edition
Printed papers from My Mind's Eye and
Daisy D's Paper Co.; rub-on transfers from
Rusty Pickle and Making Memories.

TREASURE EACH DAY

Use coloured photo pencils to draw attention to portions of a black-and-white photo.

Design | Kathleen Paneitz

Materials

Card stock: white, pale green
Sentiment rub-on transfer
Wallet-size black-and-white photo
Yellow gingham ribbon
Photo painting pencils
Pre-colour treatment photo spray
Paper adhesive

Instructions

Form a 5 x 4¼-inch top-fold card from pale green card stock. Insert a piece of gingham ribbon through inside of card; tie into a bow on front of card and trim ends.

Following manufacturer's instructions, apply a layer of pre-colour treatment photo spray to photo. Add colour with photo painting pencils; adhere to white card stock. Trim white card stock leaving a small border and adhere over gingham ribbon. Apply rub-on transfer below photo. ■

TREASURE EACH DAY

Treasure Each Day
Rub-on transfer from Making Memories; photo painting pencils and pre-colour treatment photo spray from Brandess-Kalt-Aetna Group Inc.

MOMENT

A black-and-white photo adds drama to a simple card design.

Design | Sheryl Busse

Materials

Card stock: brown, blue, light tan
Coordinating printed papers: blue swirl, brown striped
3¼-inch-square black-and-white photo
⅜-inch-wide brown grosgrain ribbon
The Good Life acrylic rubber stamp set (includes "moment")
Brown dye ink pad
Pewter photo hanger with brad
1⁄16-inch hole punch
Paper glue

Instructions

Form a 4¼ x 5½-inch side-fold card from brown card stock. Adhere blue swirl printed paper to card; trim and ink edges. Cut a 1 x 5½-inch piece of brown striped paper; ink edges and adhere to centre of card front.

Adhere photo to blue card stock; trim a small border and adhere to card as shown. Stamp "moment" on light tan card stock; cut a 2½ x ¾-inch rectangle around word. Ink edges and adhere to blue card stock; trim a small border. Ink edges. Use brad to attach hanger to right end of rectangle. Tie ribbon onto hanger; trim ribbon ends. Adhere rectangle to bottom of card. ■

Moment

Printed papers, ribbon, photo hanger, rubber stamp set and ink pad from Close To My Heart.

LIFE'S DETOURS

Create this unique encouragement card with a simple sentiment and street sign photo.

Design | Alice Golden

Materials

Premade bifold blue card with envelope
License plates printed paper
Photo of "Detour" road sign
Black distress ink pad
"discover" metal sign
2 translucent halo button snaps
Black wax-coated linen thread
Black marker (optional)
1/8-inch hole punch
Removable tape
Paper glue
Computer, printer paper and matte-finish photo paper

Instructions

Use a computer to generate "Detours happen. Remember your destination." on card front by first printing text on printer paper. Then use removable tape to attach the card to the printer paper, lining up the placement of the text to where it should appear on card front. Use removable tape to keep card closed. Print words on card front.

Option: Hand-print the words on card front with black marker. Ink card edges.

Use a computer to print road-sign image on photo paper or use actual photo. Trim image to fit on top portion of card. Place image on card front to determine where it needs to be cut in half. Cut image in half and adhere one half to each side of card.

Adhere "discover" sign to right side of card. Punch a 1/8-inch hole through each side of card below image. Attach a button snap through each hole. Tie a piece of wax-coated thread to one of the button snaps; wrap thread around both snaps to secure shut. Trim thread to desired length.

To decorate envelope, use envelope as a template to cut a piece of license plates printed paper to fit inside envelope. Slip paper inside and adhere, applying adhesive to top edge only. This will prevent paper from crinkling when folded. ∎

DETOUR

discover

Detours happen.
Remember your destination.

Life's Detours
Card from Die Cuts With A View; printed paper from Karen Foster
Design; halo button snaps from Cloud 9 Design; metal sign from
Making Memories; distress ink pad from Ranger Industries Inc.

SHARP TURNS AHEAD

A common roadside sign makes a real statement when partnered with a thought-provoking sentiment.

Design | Alice Golden

Materials

Printed papers: golden-yellow metal print, road print
White envelope to fit a 4⅛ x 4⅜-inch card
Photo of road sign
Black distress ink pad
Black marker (optional)
Adhesive foam tape
Removable tape
Glue stick
Computer with scanner and printer
Printer paper and matte-finish photo paper

Instructions

Form a 4⅛ x 4⅜-inch top-fold card from golden yellow metal printed paper. Use a computer to generate "A bend in the road is not the end of the road ... unless you fail to make the turn. —Unknown" by printing the quotation first on a sheet of printer paper. Use removable tape to attach card to same sheet of printer paper, lining card up with text to ensure correct position. Run through printer again. Remove card from printer paper. *Option: Hand-write quotation on card with black marker.*

Use a photo of a road sign or if desired, scan photo and print on photo paper. Cut photo to desired size to fit left side of card. Ink edges. Use adhesive foam tape to adhere photo to card.

To decorate envelope, use envelope as a template to cut a piece of road printed paper that will fit inside top envelope flap. Adhere paper inside envelope, applying adhesive to top edge only. This will prevent paper from crinkling when folded. ■

A bend in the road is not the end of the road... unless you fail to make the turn.
- UNKNOWN

Sharp Turns Ahead
Printed papers from Cloud 9 Design and Karen Foster Design; ink pad from Ranger Industries Inc.

VINTAGE JOURNEY

Create quick and easy photo greeting cards with reprints of vintage family photos.

Design | Linda Beeson

Materials

Card stock: white, black
Newsprint printed paper
Vintage car photo
"journey" rubber stamp
"enjoy" and "vintage" rub-on transfers
Clear dimensional square stickers
Brown dye ink pad
Chalk ink pads: black, brown, golden yellow
White or silver pen (optional)
2 large black hooks (from hook-and-eye sets)
Twine
Thread: light brown, dark brown
Sandpaper
Sewing needle
Sewing machine with reddish-brown thread
Glue stick

Instructions

To remove shiny coating from photo, run photo under water, getting front and back wet. Allow to dry. Roughly sand photo in various directions. Rub chalk inks over surface and along edges of sanded photo. Mat photo onto black card stock; machine-sew a zigzag stitch around photo edges with light brown thread. Mat again onto newsprint printed paper; rub black chalk ink on edges.

Use brown ink to stamp "journey" onto white card stock; trim a rectangle around word and rub chalk inks on entire surface and along edges. Thread sewing needle with dark brown thread and sew a hook on left and right sides of "journey" rectangle. Referring to photo, glue rectangle at an angle on bottom of photo. Tie a piece of twine to each hook; wrap ends around to reverse side of newsprint printed paper. Form an 8 x 5-inch top-fold card from black card stock; adhere assembled piece onto card front.

Transfer "enjoy" in upper left corner of photo; transfer "vintage" in lower right corner of photo. Attach clear square stickers on top of "vintage."

Use a white or silver pen to write on reverse side of postcard or cut a piece of white card stock and adhere on reverse side for writing area. ■

Vintage Journey

Rubber stamp from American Art Stamp; rub-on transfers from Chatterbox Inc.; square stickers from Making Memories; chalk ink pads from Clearsnap Inc.

TREASURE & TRUST

Honour a true friend with a card that celebrates all the traits that make her special!

Design | Mary Ayres

Materials

Card stock: white, blue, green, pink, yellow
Coordinating striped paper
3½ x 4½-inch photo
Friend sentiments rub-on transfers
8½ inches ⅝-inch-wide pink grosgrain ribbon
Blue dye ink pad
Buttons: pastel pink, yellow, blue
White embroidery floss
Sewing needle
Craft sponge
Rotary tool and scoring blade
Pinking shears
Fabric adhesive

Instructions

Form an 8 x 5-inch top-fold card from white card stock. Apply blue ink to edges of card with a craft sponge. Transfer "Friends" sentiment onto white card stock; cut a 1 x 1¾-inch rectangle around word and apply blue ink to edges. Glue rectangle to upper left side of card.

Cut a 3¾ x 4¾-inch rectangle from white card stock; apply blue ink to edges. Adhere photo to rectangle and glue rectangle to card. Cut a rectangle from striped paper that measures 2½ x 7¾ inches. Referring to photo, trim rectangle diagonally so that height on left side of trimmed rectangle measures approximately ¾ inch. Apply blue ink to edges and adhere to bottom of card.

Trim ends of ribbon with pinking shears; glue across top of striped paper. With sewing needle and floss, thread each button; knot floss on top and trim ends. Glue one button to each ribbon end.

Transfer four sentiments onto white card stock; cut ½-inch-wide rectangles around words, leaving extra space on left side for buttons. Apply blue ink to edges. Cut rectangles from coloured card stock that measure ⅛ inch larger on all sides than word rectangles; apply blue ink to edges. Glue card-stock rectangles to back of words; glue a button to each rectangle and glue rectangles diagonally underneath photo. ∎

Treasure & Trust

Striped paper from K&Company; rub-on transfers from Royal & Langnickel; Fabri-Tac adhesive from Beacon Adhesives Inc.

BLISS

The use of a fun pet photo creates the ideal centrepiece on this simple greeting card.

Design | Louise Granlund

Materials

Card stock: white, lavender
Printed paper with zigzags and swirls
5¼ x 2⅞-inch photo
White business-size envelope
Chipboard shapes: small flower, "b"
Alphabet rub-on transfers
Sandpaper
Paper glue

Instructions

Form an 8½ x 4-inch top-fold card from white card stock. Cut an 8¼ x 3¾-inch piece of printed paper that includes a zigzag along left edge and swirls along right edge; adhere to card front. Adhere photo to lavender card stock; trim a small border. Adhere to card as shown.

Lightly sand chipboard shapes; adhere flower to upper left corner of photo and "b" to right side of photo. Apply alphabet rub-on transfers to card next to chipboard "b" to finish the word "bLiss."

Decorate envelope as desired with printed paper. ■

Bliss
Printed paper from Adornit/Carolee's Creations; chipboard shapes and rub-on transfers from K&Company.

RELAX

*Create a simple but stylish greeting
card using mirror-image photos.*

Design | Mary Ayres

Materials

Black card stock
Printed papers: light green, dark green
2 x 3-inch colour photos: 2 of the same subject,
    2 of the same subject printed in mirror image
Black fine-tip marker
1¾-inch silver oval bookplate
Brads: decorative square, 2 antique mini
Fine sandpaper
Hole punches: ⅛-inch, 1⁄16-inch
Sewing machine with black thread
Paper glue
Computer and printer (optional)

Instructions

Form a 5 x 8-inch side-fold card from black card stock.

Cut a 4¾ x 6½-inch piece of dark green printed paper;
sand edges and glue to front of card ⅛ inch from top edge.

Lightly draw a horizontal line across centre of dark green
printed paper; draw another line down vertical centre.
Machine-stitch over lines to edges of dark green printed
paper using black thread and a straight stitch.

Sand edges of photos. Adhere photos in mirror-image
positions inside stitched quadrants.

Punch a ⅛-inch hole in centre of photo panel; mount
decorative brad in hole.

Hand-print, or use a computer to generate, "Relax" on
light green printed paper to fit in oval bookplate. Trim
around word; adhere to back of bookplate. Punch 1⁄16-inch
holes for mounting bookplate near bottom of card; mount
bookplate with antique mini brads. ■

Relax Card
Printed papers from BasicGrey; Zip Dry
Paper Glue from Beacon Adhesives Inc.

WHAT'S UP?

Drop a note to say hello and catch up with friends when you send this fun-loving photo card.

Design | Kathleen Paneitz

Materials

Green textured card stock
Pastel striped printed paper
3½ x 5¼-inch photo
Mixed white rub-on transfers
Metal flower brad
Paper glue

Instructions

Form a 4¼ x 5½-inch top-fold card from green card stock.

Cut printed paper to 1 x 5¼ inches; adhere near right front side of card. Adhere photo to front of card, overlapping printed paper slightly.

Apply rub-on transfers to top of photo to spell "What's up?" Attach flower brad to lower right corner of card front. ■

What's Up?
Printed paper from BasicGrey; rub-on transfers from Making Memories; metal flower brad from Creative Imaginations; Zip Dry Paper Glue from Beacon Adhesives.Inc.

MISSING YOU

The "miss you" sentiment combines with a photo of sad puppy-dog eyes to succinctly state your thoughts.

Design | Susan Stringfellow

Materials
Photo of puppy
Card stock: neutral, black
Neutral diamond-pattern printed paper
Neutral fabric paper
Decorative rub-on transfer
Ink pads: light brown, black
Fine sandpaper
Glue stick
Computer and printer

Instructions
Form a 7 x 5-inch top-fold card from neutral card stock. Ink edges of card with light brown and black inks.

Cut a 6¾ x 4¾-inch piece of printed paper. Sand the edges and ink with light brown ink. Centre and adhere printed paper to card.

Trim photo to 5⅞ x 3⅞ inches. Mat photo on black card stock; trim, leaving narrow border. Centre and adhere photo to card.

Use computer to generate "missing you" three times on fabric paper to fit on a strip 5 x ½ inch; trim strip to size and adhere up left edge of card. *Option: Letter fabric paper by hand with a black permanent fine-tip marker, or use black alphabet rub-on transfers.*

Apply decorative rub-on transfer to lower right corner of card, overlapping photo. ■

Missing You

Printed paper from The Paper Loft; fabric paper from me & my BIG ideas; rub-on transfer from Heidi Swapp/Advantus Corp.; inks from Ranger Industries Inc. and Tsukineko Inc.

SNOWMOBILING DAD

Paper weaving turns a coloured photo reprint into a card designed to honour Dad.

Design | Lorine Mason

Materials
Card stock: red textured, black
Copy of colour photo
Square alphabet tiles to spell "DAD"
4 nickel mini brads
1/16-inch hole punch
Adhesive foam squares
Paper glue

Instructions
Form a 6 x 6¼-inch side-fold card from red textured card stock.

Trim photo to fit on front of card. Mark vertical centre of photo. Measuring outward, mark photo into five vertical sections. They need not be exactly even; be sure to leave main image intact.

Cut photo apart along lines. Glue top edge of each strip to front of card.

Cut several 1/16-inch-wide strips from red textured card stock. Weave red strips through the photo strips as shown without obscuring the main image. Trim ends of strips and adhere to front of card with paper glue.

Adhere bottom edge of photo strips to front of card. Frame photo with ¼-inch-wide strips cut from black card stock; adhere with paper glue. Punch 1/16-inch holes in corners of frame; mount mini brads in holes.

Adhere letter tiles to front of card with adhesive foam squares. ■

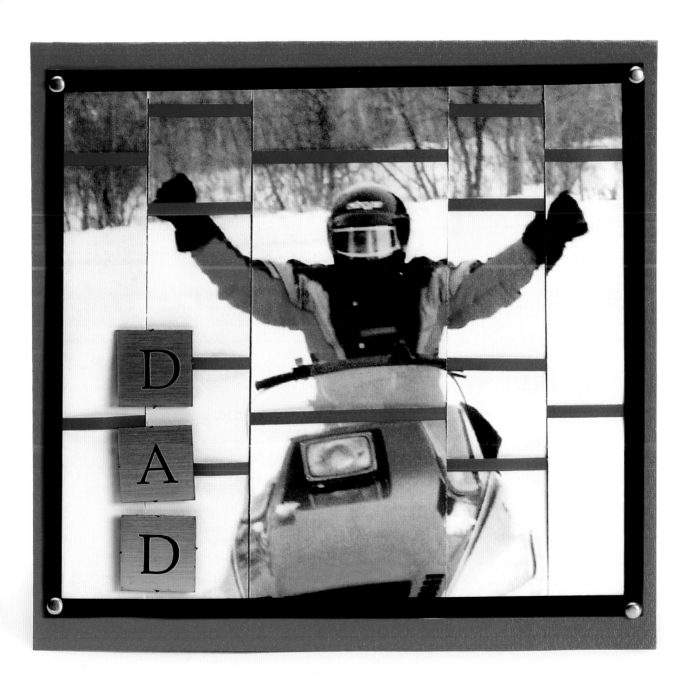

Snowmobiling Dad

SOLITUDE

Send thoughts of inspiration and encouragement with this photo framed in a window card.

Design | Janice Musante

Materials

Card stock: olive green, black
Kraft paper
3½ x 3½-inch nature photo
Envelope to fit a 4¼ x 5½-inch card
Rub-on transfers: "Solitude," "Memories"
3 pressed flowers
16½ inches green textured yarn
Thin quartz slice
Clear micro beads
Dye ink pads: green, brown
Distressing tool(s)
Die-cutting machine with SureCut Card,
    Window #3 die (#12598)
Tapestry needle
Craft knife
Double-sided adhesive sheets
Paper adhesive

Instructions

Die-cut a window card with photo mount from olive green card stock. Position photo inside card so it shows through window and adhere photo to card. Adhere photo mount on top of photo as a frame.

Apply "Solitude" rub-on transfer to quartz slice. Use quartz slice as a template to cut a piece from double-sided adhesive sheet with craft knife; attach adhesive to bottom of quartz and adhere to lower right corner of front of card as shown. Apply "Memories" rub-on transfer to upper right corner of front of card. Tear two thin strips of black card stock to fit along left side of card front; adhere one strip to left side of card front and the other to right side of left panel inside card.

Lay a flower on double-sided adhesive; use craft knife to cut around flower. Use this shape to cut a second piece from double-sided adhesive. Attach one adhesive piece to bottom of flower; attach flower to upper left corner of card front. Attach second piece of adhesive on top of the flower. Pour micro beads onto the adhesive, pressing them into the adhesive.

Thread needle with yarn and hand-stitch yarn onto card-stock strip inside card. Repeat to hand-stitch another piece of yarn to card-stock strip on card front. Use distressing tool(s) to add texture to front and inside of card. Ink edges and inside of card. Apply "simple things" rub-on transfer below photo inside card.

Carefully take apart pre-made envelope and use as a template to cut an envelope from kraft paper; score and fold to form envelope flaps, but do not assemble yet. Tear a small piece of black card stock; adhere to what will be bottom of envelope front. In the same manner as for card, adhere two flowers to lower right area of envelope front and pour micro beads on top of flowers. Hand-stitch a piece of yarn to card-stock strip. Assemble envelope. ■

Solitude

Quartz slice from Zion Rock & Gem; rub-on transfers from Making Memories, Jo-Ann Stores Inc. and me & my BIG ideas; micro beads from Halcraft USA Inc.; distressing tool kit from Making Memories; die-cutting machine and die from Ellison; Zip Dry Paper Glue from Beacon Adhesives Inc.

INDEX

INDEX

Holidays

Pocket of Love, 40

Easter Tulips, 46

Decorating Eggs, 48

Cherished Memories, 50

Enjoy Each Moment, 52

Love of My Life, 43

Trick or Treat, 54

Snowy Arbour, 58

Jingle All The Way, 60

Giving Thanks, 56

INDEX

Seasons

INDEX

GENERAL INFORMATION

METRIC CONVERSION CHARTS

METRIC CONVERSIONS

yards	x	.9144	=	metres (m)
yards	x	91.44	=	centimetres (cm)
inches	x	2.54	=	centimetres (cm)
inches	x	25.40	=	millimetres (mm)
inches	x	.0254	=	metres (m)

centimetres	x	.3937	=	inches
metres	x	1.0936	=	yards

INCHES INTO MILLIMETRES & CENTIMETRES (Rounded off slightly)

inches	mm	cm	inches	cm	inches	cm	inches	cm
1/8	3	0.3	5	12.5	21	53.5	38	96.5
1/4	6	0.6	5 1/2	14	22	56	39	99
3/8	10	1	6	15	23	58.5	40	101.5
1/2	13	1.3	7	18	24	61	41	104
5/8	15	1.5	8	20.5	25	63.5	42	106.5
3/4	20	2	9	23	26	66	43	109
7/8	22	2.2	10	25.5	27	68.5	44	112
1	25	2.5	11	28	28	71	45	114.5
1 1/4	32	3.2	12	30.5	29	73.5	46	117
1 1/2	38	3.8	13	33	30	76	47	119.5
1 3/4	45	4.5	14	35.5	31	79	48	122
2	50	5	15	38	32	81.5	49	124.5
2 1/2	65	6.5	16	40.5	33	84	50	127
3	75	7.5	17	43	34	86.5		
3 1/2	90	9	18	46	35	89		
4	100	10	19	48.5	36	91.5		
4 1/2	115	11.5	20	51	37	94		

We have a sweet lineup of cookbooks
with plenty more in the oven

www.companyscoming.com

FREE recipes and cooking tips
Exclusive cookbook offers
Preview new titles
Find titles no longer in stores

FREE online newsletter - Subscribe today!

Company's
Coming